About the Author

I.V. Hilliard is the Senior Pastor of New Light Christian Center Church ("One Church, Multiple locations") in North, South, East and West Houston; Beaumont and Austin, Texas. His unwavering compassion, along with his faithfulness to build PURPOSE, POWER, and PRAISE into God's people, will continue yielding great results in the Kingdom of God. He is seen on television across the nation and ministers all over the world, carrying the powerful message of faith. He is married to Bridget Hilliard who serves with him faithfully in ministry.

The Maximized Life Journey:

52 Days to Victorious Living!

The Maximized Life Journey:

52 Days to Victorious Living!

by

I.V. Hilliard

Scripture quotations marked NKJ are from the New King James Version. Copyright © 1982 by Thomas Nelson, Inc. Used by permission. All rights reserved. Scripture quotations marked NIV are taken from the HOLY BIBLE, NEW INTERNATIONAL VERSION®, Copyright © 1973, 1978, 1984 by the International Bible Society. Used by permission of Zondervan. All rights reserved. Scripture quotations marked MSG are taken from The Message. Copyright © 1993, 1994, 1995, 1996, 2000, 2001, 2002. Used by permission of NavPress Publishing Group. Scripture quotations marked AMP are taken from the Amplified® Bible, Copyright © 1954, 1958, 1962, 1964, 1965, 1987 by The Lockman Foundation. Used by permission. Scripture quotations marked KJV are taken from the King James Version. Scripture quotations marked NCV are from the New Century Version. Copyright © 2005 by Thomas Nelson, Inc. Used by permission. All rights reserved. Scripture quotations marked CEV are from the Contemporary English Version. Copyright © 1995 by American Bible Society. Used by permission. All rights reserved. Scripture quotations marked ESV are from the English Standard Version. Copyright © 2001 by Crossway Bibles, a division of Good News Publishers. Used by permission. All rights reserved. Scripture quotations marked NLT are from the New Living Translation. Copyright © 1996, 2004 by Tyndale Charitable Trust. Used by permission. All rights reserved.

Emphasis within Scripture quotations is the author's own. Please note that Light Publications/New Spectrum Media Concept style capitalizes all pronouns in Scripture that refer to God. The name satan and related references are not capitalized intentionally.

This book is protected by the copyright laws of the United States of America. This book may not be copied or reprinted for commercial gain or profit. No part of this publication may be reproduced, distributed, or transmitted in any form or by any means or stored in a database or retrieval system without prior written permission of the Publisher.

The use of short quotations or occasional page copying for personal or group study is permitted and encouraged. Permission will be granted upon request.

The Maximized Life Journey: 52 Days to Victorious Living!
Copyright © 2009 by Ira Van Hilliard
ISBN 13: 978-1881357-90-2

Published by Light Publications/New Spectrum Media Concepts
PO Box 670167
Houston, TX 77267

Visit our Websites at www.newlight.org & www.newspectrummedia.com

Printed in the United States of America

Table of Contents

Acknowledgments i
Introduction 1

REVELATION OF PURPOSE

Day 1 – Living on Purpose 5
Day 2 – Never Walk Alone 11

REALITY OF PROBLEMS

Day 3 – It's Not You 17
Day 4 – But It's About You 21
Day 5 – More Choices that Matter 25

RESPECT FOR PARTNERSHIPS

Day 6 – The Power of Partnerships 29
Day 7 – Respecting Partnerships 35
Day 8 – Maximizing Partnerships 39

RESOURCEFULNESS PRINCIPLES

Day 9 – It Starts with Your Faith 45
Day 10 – It's Alright to Ask 51
Day 11 – Learning to Believe 57
Day 12 – Words and Works 63
Day 13 – Be Obedient & Patient 69
Day 14 – Don't Stop Believing 73
Day 15 – Faith Works 77

REGIMEN OF PRAYER

Day 16 – Stop the Prayer Blockers 83
Day 17 – Prayer Works 89
Day 18 – It's All Good 95

REVELATION OF PROSPERITY

Day 19 – Be Prosperity Minded 101
Day 20 – Prosperity Explained..105
Day 21 – Prosperity with Purpose..111
Day 22 – Strategies for Prosperity..115
Day 23 – Prospering on Purpose..119

RESPONSIBILITY FOR PLANNING

Day 24 – Mastering the Mechanics..125
Day 25 – Managing Your Problems...131
Day 26 – It's Not God's Fault 135
Day 27 – Get Ready for Fresh Fire...141
Day 28 – Overcoming Inferior Thoughts..................................145
Day 29 – Renewing Your Mind..149
Day 30 – Maximizing Your Mind...153
Day 31 – Shaping Your Conscience 157
Day 32 – Maximizers Meditate 163
Day 33 – Mechanics of Meditation..169
Day 34 – Garbage in, Garbage Out 175
Day 35 – Take Out the Trash..181
Day 36 – 12 Steps to Success 187
Day 37 – Take the DARE...191

REVOLUTIONARY PLANTING
Day 38 – Live Generously 195
Day 39 – Open the Windows 201
Day 40 – Seed Faith Giving 207
Day 41 – Honoring God's Servants 213
Day 42 – Vow and Pay 219

RIGHTEOUS PROCLAMATIONS
Day 43 – Your Words Matter 225
Day 44 – The Force of Faith 231
Day 45 – The Word Works 235

RESOLVE OF PERSISTENCE
Day 46 – Don't Give Up 241
Day 47 – Be Diligent 247
Day 48 – No More Excuses 251

RADICAL PRAISE
Day 49 – Maximizing Your Praise 257
Day 50 – A Lifestyle of Praise 263

RECIPROCAL PROMOTION
Day 51 – Maximizers on a Mission 269
Day 52 – Pass it On 275

Additional Resources 281

Acknowledgments

The Maximized Life is a journey in which many people make significant contributions along the way. With gratitude, I acknowledge those persons who have been instrumental in the journey on which you are about to embark.

To my Heavenly Father: You inspired my Maximized Life Journey and empowered me to achieve it.

To my wife, Bridget: For your love and support; having you as my partner in marriage and ministry has made this journey a great joy!

To my children and grandchildren: For serving God with passion and taking the Gospel to the next generation, you all are well on your way to the Maximized Life.

To my New Light Church family (North, South, East, West, Austin and Beaumont): For 25 years of outstanding commitment to maximizing our God-given assignment! I could not have asked for a better church!

To my staff: For your diligence and faithfulness to serve God with excellence; there is no limit to what we can accomplish.

To my co-collaborators, Johnathan Briggs, Trevón Gross, and Matthew Haskell: For your partnership that made this project possible.

Introduction

You picked up this book for a reason! It could be because you were intrigued by the title or the prospect of gaining victory in your life. You may have wondered if all this can be done in 52 days. Regardless of the reason, this is a destiny appointment! God has a plan for your life! And you are days away from learning your purpose and taking your life to a whole different level.

Why write a book like this? Well, I have a story to tell and truth to impart! I grew up in the Fifth Ward of Houston, Texas. It was a bona fide ghetto! The prospects for my life were not stellar because I did not come from wealth: I was not educated in exclusive preparatory academies; I was not socialized around those with silver spoons. I had a lot of dreams but very little exposure to strategies that would bring success in my life. However, I was taught three key lessons in my life, which formed the foundation of my success.

First, God must be a central part of my life. This has been a growing relationship since my childhood. My decision to surrender my life to the love of Jesus Christ set the stage for the phenomenal success I have enjoyed. The Bible, God's Word, has been the ultimate Truth for my family and me. Its standards have shaped my character and its principles have guided my actions for more than 40 years, and I am the better because of it. Let me tell you, from the outset of this journey, you will never be able to achieve your highest potential unless you acknowledge your Creator!

Second, I was taught to be diligent. Hard work is a lost attribute these days. Many are looking for quick success and easy-street living with no real investment. From what I have learned, expectations like these are, at best, unsustainable and, at worst, impossible! You will always get out of life what you invest into it.

Introduction

Life is just waiting to be maximized if you will be diligent. If you awake each day with purpose and a plan, you can revolutionize your situation. It does not matter what state your life is in! It does not matter how many faults and failings you have had. You can win with the hand you have been dealt! Diligence will make the difference.

And, third, I was taught to identify role models and respect their time. While I did not have many examples around me of the type and quality of life I dreamed about, I knew that if I studied successful people and learned from their lives, I would achieve all my dreams. Along the way, God orchestrated destiny appointments where I met people who were critical to my development. Realizing the divine nature of these interactions, I was intentional about maximizing these relationships. I have reaped tremendous benefit from the investments they made in my life and the respect I gave to the information they imparted and the examples they set. I give honor to these people on whose wisdom my life has been built!

I desire to pass on the Truth that I have learned and pay back the investment that others have made in my life by sharing with you the principles for living the Maximized Life.

How do you Maximize Your Life?

Maximizing life is making a quality choice to embrace God's best by living a disciplined life with a positive, progressive, and persistent attitude, which allows you to overcome all handicaps, hardships, and setbacks without bitterness. This Maximized Life Journey will give you the tools and strategies to win in life in spite of less than optimal conditions. Whether it is your marriage, your career, your family, or your entire life, you can win and see all your

Maximized Life Journey: 52 Days to Victorious Living!

dreams maximized! Let me show you how. This 52-day journey will take you there!

So why 52 days? After all, it only takes 21 days to form a new habit. Why so long? Well, a significant victory was accomplished in the Bible in that period of time. Nehemiah had received a report of the deteriorated state of Jerusalem's walls and the deplorable state of the people who lived there. He knew that regardless of the condition, he could bring hope to the people and rebuild the walls. God took him on an exciting journey to do what had not been done before. Along this journey, Nehemiah received great favor and faced fierce opposition, yet he would not give up! Through all kinds of obstacles, Nehemiah forged on. And 52 days later, the walls were rebuilt! Victory was achieved!

The same will be true in your life—if you take this Maximized Life Journey seriously!

Each day you will have a reading to focus your thoughts and teach you a Maximized Life truth. Please read each chapter one day at a time. You will miss the impact if you try to rush the journey. Dedicate your mornings to read the chapter. This will give you the entire day to interact with the material you have learned.

Each day's reading will end with what I call a *Maximized Prayer*. It is your way to accept what you have read. Pray this prayer sincerely and you will see the effects daily. After you have read the chapter, there will be *Maximizing Moments*. In this section, you will answer pointed questions, which will assist you in evaluating your life and making the necessary adjustments to adopt what you have read. (I encourage you to get the Maximized Life

Introduction

Journey Passport. It will give you more assistance in capturing your thoughts and documenting your progress.)

Last, there is a *Maximizing Mantra*. A mantra is a commonly repeated phrase. These are confessions, which will help give you a new Maximizer's vocabulary. As you will learn, your mouth plays a key role in your success. Repeat these phrases often during the day; you will find your thoughts turning in new and exciting directions—towards maximizing, not minimizing, life!

My prayer for you during this journey is that you will discover what I have discovered: Life is best when it is maximized!

Welcome to the *Maximized Life Journey*—your path to victory!

I. V. Hilliard
Founder/Senior Pastor
New Light Christian Center Church
Houston, TX

Day 1 – Living on Purpose

*"For we are His workmanship,
created in Christ Jesus for good works,
which God prepared beforehand
that we should walk in them."*
Ephesians 2:10 (NKJ)

The day has arrived! This is the day that you change your life forever! No matter what challenges you are facing or problems that you need to solve, you hold in your hands a tool to produce lasting improvements in your life! Just as Nehemiah was able to rebuild the walls of Jerusalem, so you will rebuild the walls of your life, which will cause you to live in a state of complete peace.

As you begin this 52-day journey, it is important to begin with purpose. There are many books on purpose and how to find it. These books teach you how to know what your purpose is. However, knowing your purpose and understanding your purpose are two different things. Today and tomorrow you will gain an understanding of the purpose for your life. The Maximized Life Journey is rooted in your ability to understand your purpose.

From a biblical perspective, when you understand a concept, it becomes a revelation to you. So today I want you to gain the revelation of purpose. Once you understand something, then you have the ability to act on it. You can never act on something that you do not understand. (In fact, God can never hold you accountable for something that you do not understand.) The Bible says, "*Wisdom is the principal thing; Therefore get wisdom. And in all your getting, get understanding*" (Proverbs 4:7 NKJ).

Revelation is an understanding of the plan of God at your level of comprehension for which you are accountable. This is revelation. Revelation cancels doubt. If you continue in the Word of God, you will get revelation and then be free. *"And you will know the truth, and the truth will set you free"* (John 8:34 NLT). Information challenges your thinking, but revelation changes your character. That's why you must get a revelation of your purpose.

There are five spiritual things that are put into motion when you receive revelation. The first is **Divine Definition,** which simply means you know who you are. Next, revelation causes **Divine Development,** which means that you become the best that you can be. Then, **Divine Deliverance** takes place, which means you are delivered from the power of darkness, doubt, and degradation that can discourage you on your journey. (You are not bound by your past, but you are working on your future.) Also, there is **Divine Delegation,** which means that you have authority over every obstacle and hindrance that keeps you from being what God created you to do. Last, you are given **Divine Dominion,** which means you possess the ability to operate the way God intended. On this journey, the first revelation (understanding) that you need is your purpose.

Purpose is defined in the original intent of a thing. Purpose resides in the mind of the maker. Only the maker of an object defines the purpose of that object. God established humanity's purpose from the beginning of creation. If you have ever wondered what your purpose is, here is the simplified answer: to exist for the benefit of others. You were not created to pursue your own passions and desires. You were created to be a blessing to others. Thus, your purpose is always fulfilled through giving. Your life should add to the lives of others and to the earth. Your existence is validated through the impact you have on another's life. Until you

Day 1 - Living on Purpose

have made an uncommon contribution, your existence is unnecessary!

Take, for instance, a chair. The chair was created to provide comfortable seating by holding the weight of a person. The chair is not fulfilling its purpose if no one is sitting in it. In like fashion, for the Believer, attaining money, possessions, titles, and degrees will not satisfy you so long as those things are not used to the benefit of others.

The Bible says, "*God created human beings; He created them godlike, reflecting God's nature*" (Genesis 1:27 MSG). You were created with the ability to make things happen and to succeed. Failure and quitting are not your purpose. In fact, those things feel bad to you because they are against your very nature. God created you to be like Him! You should not fail. You should not lose. You should not give up. These are all against God's nature in you. Your life becomes praise to God as you live out your purpose, ==as you rise each day and discover new ways to enhance the lives of others. God gets glory from this==! Before praise ever comes from your lips, it should come from your life.

So why were you created? You were created to represent God in the earth. As God's representative, you are charged with caring for the things He has entrusted to you. You should be a good steward (manager) of the gifts and talents that God has entrusted to you. And, yes, you do have gifts and talents that are on the inside that are waiting to be discovered and used. The sooner you come into the revelation of your purpose, the sooner others will be blessed also.

As a joint heir with Christ, we are to demonstrate His Lordship in the earth. This speaks to our authority. As children of

Revelation of Purpose

God, we have been delegated the authority and the ability to have dominion in the earth. We must access and appropriate the power of God to overcome frustration, fear, disbelief, sickness, and poverty—anything that threatens the Maximized Life that Jesus died to give you! All this power is available to you for the asking.

The first decision that must be settled is your relationship with God. Are you in God's family?

Being in God's family is always a purposeful, conscious act of your will. If you're not careful, you'll dismiss Scripture and assume a relationship with God is inherited or transposed from Christian relatives or that a person's spiritual status is based on a specific church denomination rather than on Christ alone. Or, you'll base your relationship with God on a personal moral compass too weak to compare with the sacrifice of Jesus Christ, God's son. Relationship with God cannot be attained through any good work of humanity. In fact, Ephesians 2:8-9 says, *"For by grace are ye saved through faith; and that not of yourselves: it is the gift of God: Not of works, lest any man should boast"* (NKJ).

Very simply, you only need to believe in Jesus Christ, the Messiah. When you believe, you confess who you are: a Believer in Christ—a Christian. Don't confess with your mouth alone; confess by how you live your life. No longer are you subject to the principles of the world. Now you have the opportunity to surrender yourself to the Lordship of Christ in the Kingdom of God that can be revealed through you daily.

If you have never knowingly received Jesus as your Lord and Savior, the Maximized Prayer for today is written to give you the opportunity to pray it in sincerity of heart. As you pray this prayer, inviting the Lord Jesus into your life, your spirit will become alive

Day 1 - Living on Purpose

to God and you will enter the family of God: *"But as many as received Him, to them He gave the power to become sons of God, even to them that believe on His name"* (John 1:12 NKJ).

As a person who lives by purpose, you will be productive and leave a deposit in the earth. As a human, you are either withdrawing or making a deposit. Your purpose is to *"be fruitful and multiply"* (Genesis 1:28 KJV). Only Maximizers make deposits and replenish the earth. Take this journey seriously and you will see your purpose unfold in ways you could not have even imagined because you will be living on purpose, according to purpose!

Maximized Prayer:

Dear God, I know without Jesus I am lost. I believe the Scripture that says if I receive you as the Lord of my life that I can be saved and transformed. I believe that Jesus died on the cross and paid the penalty for my sins and mistakes. Jesus, I now give You the throne of my heart and surrender my will to You; and, from this day forward, I make a conscious effort to please You with my life. I receive the power of the Holy Spirit to help me live a life that is pleasing in Your sight. Thank you, Father. I believe that I am now a part of the family of God and You are my heavenly Father. I say now to satan and the powers of darkness, you no longer have the right to influence my thinking or interfere in my life. Jesus is now my Lord and I serve Him and only Him. Father God, thank you for saving me in Jesus' name. Amen.

Maximizing Moments:

List the reasons for which you were created. Evaluate where you are in each of these areas.

Maximizing Mantra:

I will prosper, reproduce, fill the earth, and take charge.

NOTES

Enhance the lives of others!

Day 2 – Never Walk Alone

*"Do two people walk hand in hand
if they aren't going to the same place?"*
Amos 3:3 (MSG)

You are well on your way towards maximizing your life by understanding that your life is not to be lived selfishly but selflessly. You were put on this earth for the benefit of others. There are deposits that God made in you before you were ever born, and there are people who need what God has put inside you! Can you see how important you are to God's plan? God created you to be a blessing to someone else.

Inasmuch as you matter to God, so does every other person whom God created. Imagine how powerful it must be when two Maximizers join hands and walk through life together. That's what today's reading is about: the importance of relationships—covenant relationships.

Covenant is an important word because it is the bond that holds two or more parties together; it is a solemn agreement. Covenant is binding on those who enter into the agreement. You cannot make the Maximized Life Journey alone—and you should not want to!

God created covenant relationships so that you can fulfill your purpose. Simply put, we need each other! As today's reading reminds us, two people cannot travel together unless they are headed in the same direction. You have probably lived this principle but not to your benefit. You may have people in your life today who are really not headed in the direction that you want to go. But their influence over you has caused you to put your dreams on hold to follow their path. It's time to change that!

Revelation of Purpose

God has designed for you to walk with people who are going in the direction that you are headed. For all that exists in you, you did not gain by accident. You are the sum total of the investments that you have allowed others to make in you!

Jesus cared so much about our connectedness to one another that He prayed, *"That they will all be one, just as you and I are one—as you are in me, Father, and I am in you. And may they be in us so that the world will believe you sent me"* (John 17:2 NLT). Jesus showed His covenant connection with the Father and with those to whom He had been sent. But Jesus also established His expectation for unity among His followers. God has connected you with many people throughout the years who are so much a part of who you have become. Have you maximized these relationships? Or have you neglected these God-given relationships because you were detoured by people going in a different direction?

Relationships are necessary to humanity. Relationships are not all equal, but all of them are important to our destiny. There are casual relationships that are developed when you meet people in informal, nonthreatening arenas and choose to give them access to your life. There are committed relationships with family members. There are cause relationships that you have with other Believers in the Body of Christ to advance God's Kingdom. There are commercial relationships. These are the relationships developed from your work environment. Then, there are companion relationships that you have developed throughout the course of life. Whether you acknowledge it or not, these relationships have influenced you for good or ill. However, God expects you to be the godly influence and righteous consciousness in them; and, as a result, they will give you velocity towards your destiny—The Maximized Life.

God works through all relationships. All through the Bible, you see Him working in relationships. Moses and Jethro had a covenant relationship. In this relationship, Jethro taught Moses the understanding of delegation. Moses was able to maximize his leadership ability because of this relationship.

There was the covenant relationship between Moses and Joshua. Joshua was able to learn from Moses and expand upon Moses' legacy and leadership. Another example was the relationship between Elijah and Elisha. Elijah served as a model for Elisha and set the stage for his success.

There was the relationship between Ruth and Naomi. They established a surrogate mother and daughter relationship, which was mutually beneficial. It led Naomi to peace and security and Ruth to Boaz (her husband). There are many more examples in the Bible. All of these relationships were advantageous because they had a unity of purpose: *"My dear friends, as a follower of our Lord Jesus Christ, I beg you to get along with each other. Don't take sides. Always try to agree in what you think"* (1 Corinthians 1:10 CEV). Unity of purpose within the relationship provides mutual maximum momentum for all involved.

Everyone benefits from unity of purpose. Whether it is commercial, casual, committed, or cause related, when purpose is agreed upon, those relationships assist in your Maximum Life Journey. However, if those relationships are toxic, turbulent, or traumatic, you may need to renegotiate them.

Some relationships will need to be eliminated. This may sound harsh, but it is necessary! Some people will do more to hinder your progress, and they cannot be in your life. Others, because they are categorized as committed relationships (familial), may need to be regulated; those relationships will need to be redefined. And, then, you will need to cultivate new relationships with people who have a unity of purpose. (If you are married, that relationship is crucial to your journey! Use this 52-day journey to realign your marriage so that you can establish unity of purpose and find fulfillment in your relationship. It does not matter what state your marriage is in, you can win from there!)

There are three key relationships that each Maximizer needs: a teacher, a trusted companion, and a trainee. A teacher is someone who represents the Maximized Life. This must be someone who is willing to impart principles and wisdom as you take your journey. A suitable teacher is one who has a vested interest in your success. A trusted companion is someone with whom you are on a similar Maximized Life Journey. You hold each other accountable for the lessons that you learn and implementing them in your life. You also provide encouragement on the journey! The trainee is someone who you are mentoring into the Maximized Life. You should have all three of these relationships in your life at all times.

Because relationships are so vital to your destiny, you must begin to honestly evaluate with whom you spend your time and determine their impact, positively or negatively, on your journey. In response to what you find, you will identify needed relationships (teachers, trusted companions, and trainees) that you should cultivate. God will lead you to the right people once you regulate and eliminate the negative, non-purposeful relationships in your life. The Maximized Life Journey cannot be taken alone! And you are in a good position to gain some more travelers on this journey today!

Maximized Prayer:
Father, You did not design me to take this journey alone! I thank You for bringing into my life people to help me be my best for You! I covenant with You that I will welcome them and receive from them. In Jesus' name, Amen.

Maximizing Moments:
What relationships are in your life that you need to eliminate, regulate, or cultivate?

Identify who will serve as your teacher, trusted companion, and trainee. (This may evolve over time, but this should be a starting point.)

Maximizing Mantra:
All my relationships maximize my life!

Notes

Day 3 – It's Not You

*"No test or temptation that comes your way
is beyond the course of what others have had to face."*
1 Corinthians 10:13a (MSG)

Problems are a part of the human condition. In every person's life, challenges will come. Often when these turbulent times arise, you begin to blame yourself. "Why me?" is your constant cry. Somehow, the presence of problems suggests that you are inadequate or incapable of living a Maximized Life. However, the truth is that living the Maximized Life means that you must master problems and problem solving.

Are you facing problems? It may be in your relationships, career, personal development, or finances. If you are going to be successful in overcoming the problems in your life, you must start with a positive approach.

Blaming yourself is never the best approach. When you recognize that problems are a part of life, you will make mastering problems a higher priority. The hallmark of the Maximized Life Journey is learning to solve problems. When you have mastered problem solving, you will face reversals, unexpected events, mishaps, and shortfalls with confidence. The Bible reassures you that "*no test or temptation*" has confronted you beyond what others have faced! That should encourage you! Whatever you are facing is not new! It might be new to you! But someone else has encountered the same or similar problem that you are facing.

You should never allow problems to intimidate you—no matter how large they may seem. Your attitude towards problems will determine how you handle them. Moreover, there is no challenge or roadblock that you will ever face that is bigger than the God you

Reality of Problems

serve! As a Maximizer, you will gain a new perspective on problems and how to resolve them. So how do you adjust your attitude towards problems?

First, your attitude must be adjusted on purpose. Set your mind to reevaluate the problems you are facing. This is not the time for a pity party! Problems are a call to action! Your attitude will not change until you change your actions. Fight the feelings of helplessness and overwhelm. You are uniquely designed to solve problems. Purpose in your heart that you can solve every problem that you are currently experiencing and every problem that will arise in the future. If you are facing it, you can handle it. Stand up to problems with the confidence that God will help you and you possess the ability to overcome them.

Next, you should see problems as a source of personal and professional development. When you go to the gym to exercise, an important truth is revealed. Muscle growth only comes from the presence of tension. The same is true of your maturity. Problems represent a good mental, emotional, and spiritual workout for you. There is untapped potential within you that you have never realized, and solving problems will make a demand on all of your internal resources. This is why you cannot ignore problems or be intimidated by them. You will miss an opportunity to grow in ways you did not know were possible.

Third, you should be open to mid-course corrections. Some of the problems you face will point out that a course correction is needed. In other words, problems can be warning signals for even greater challenges that can lie ahead. Solving the problem today by making a course correction can rescue you from impending larger problems. The future problems may actually cause greater

Day 3 - It's Not You

disruption if not averted. Timeliness is a part of problem solving. Procrastination can be disastrous to the Maximized Life Journey. Fear and intimidation can paralyze you and delay the solutions to your problems. Take the advice of Solomon: "*Catch us the foxes, The little foxes that spoil the vines*" (Song of Solomon 2:15 NKJ).

Also, you should have confidence that God is at work in the problem-solving process. Our reading for today informs us that our problems are common. But there is a greater assurance as well: "*All you need to remember is that God will never let you down; he'll never let you be pushed past your limit; he'll always be there to help you come through it*" (1 Corinthians 10:13 MSG). God is at work to help you through the problem, and He will also give you divine creativity to assist you in resolving the problem. (We'll talk more about this tomorrow.) Your attitude should exude confidence because you are not solving problems alone. God is at work refining skills that you did not know you had.

Last, and this should really excite you, you should know that successful problem solving leads to promotion! I have often said, "He who solves problems gets paid." This compensation comes in many forms. It may mean promotions and financial remuneration, but it also means growth and development. Moreover, because God is involved in the problem-solving process, He is evaluating our progress and stands ready to reward us for our efforts.

So, as you move towards victory in every area of your life, know that your problems are not a referendum on you! They are a part of life and you are well qualified to solve them. And, when you solve problems in your life, you will be promoted!

Reality of Problems

Maximized Prayer:
> Father, I know that what I face is not about my inadequacy. I do recognize that they are about maturing me to be who You created me to be. I am ready for this journey. In Jesus' name, Amen.

Maximizing Moments:
> In what areas have you felt a victim? Take authority over those areas and decide that you no longer will blame yourself but will intentionally plan to turn your life around.

Maximizing Mantra:
> I am an overcomer!

Day 4 – But It's About You

*"Embrace this God-life. Really embrace it,
and nothing will be too much for you."*
Mark 11:22 (MSG)

As we saw yesterday, your problems are not an assessment of you! However, they are about you! The challenges you face and the way you handle them do speak about who you are and what role God plays in your life. Your attitude and approach to problems will be a reflection of who you are.

How is it about you? It's about the choices you make once the problem has been revealed. While it is true that some of the problems you face are a call to a midcourse correction, there are times when problems just arise. And, when they do, every decision and response that you make will affect how long that problem stays and the manner in which you come through it.

Here are some deliberate choices you should make:

Choose to refocus. Problems elicit thoughts and emotions that you may not have known before. To be sure, when the unexpected happens, you are tempted to fear and doubt. These are just two of the many emotions that come rushing upon you when a problem surfaces. These emotions and thoughts can actually lead you away from the solution that you seek!

Your thought-life will be under attack during the problem-solving process. Refocusing your thinking on solving the problem is the best course of action rather than going down the paths that your emotions tread. Your emotions will lead you to fear. If you stay in a state of fear, helplessness will not be far behind. Helplessness can lead to despair, which can result in hopelessness. At this point, suicide or other irrational thoughts will overtake you! Decisions

Reality of Problems

made from fear will always take you off course! Fear hinders God's ability to help you. At various points in the Bible, when people were confronted with overwhelming situations, messengers from God encouraged them with these simple words, "Fear Not!" These words should be in your problem-solving vocabulary. Repeat them to yourself often.

Whatever the problem, stay focused like a laser on its resolution. Focus is a powerful tool because when you focus on something, it will make visible things you never saw before. Think of it this way: When you glance at a painting, you may get a glimpse of the design and the features. However, if you linger and examine the painting, you will begin to see a lot of detail: You will see the brush strokes, the aging, the colors, etc. Here is how Scripture relates this: "*The light of the body is the eye: if therefore thine eye be single, thy whole body shall be full of light*" (Matthew 6:22 KJV). Refocusing will give you the clarity you need to develop a plan to solve whatever is facing you!

Choose to remember. As the pressure mounts, and it will, you should be anchored in a fundamental truth: "What really matters has not changed." Problems seem to present a false reality that everything has changed. Yet those things that matter most are still the same. God's promises are still the same. God promised Joshua, "*In the same way I was with Moses, I'll be with you. I won't give up on you; I won't leave you*" (Joshua 1:5 MSG). The Book of Hebrews reminds us, "*I will not in any way fail you nor give you up nor leave you without support. [I will] not, [I will] not, [I will] not in any degree leave you helpless nor forsake nor let [you] down (relax My hold on you)! [Assuredly not!]*" (Hebrews 13:5 AMP). When the feelings of loneliness and abandonment arise, these truths must anchor your thoughts! Remind yourself of God's promises because those are the things that matter and they have not changed!

Choose to rehearse. There is power in God's Word. The creative power in God's Word is seen in Genesis. At every point, when God wanted results, He spoke, "*Let there be...*" and "*There was!*" The same is true for the Believer. We learn an important principle from Scripture: "*At the mouth of two witnesses, or at the mouth of three witnesses, shall the matter be established*" (Deuteronomy 19:15 KJV). When you are battling the challenges, there will be two voices: one from God and one from the devil. You get the choice to speak life or death over your situation. You become the deciding witness. You will either speak to your destiny or against it: "*The tongue can bring death or life; those who love to talk will reap the consequences*" (Proverbs 18:21 NLT). Confession (a verbal affirmation) is a lifestyle that you will learn on Day 43. Develop the discipline to speak God's Word repeatedly. Never speak your doubts or fears!

Choose to refocus! Choose to remember! Choose to rehearse! These are quality choices. You will learn more tomorrow.

Maximized Prayer:
Father, You are the greatest Problem Solver! I trust Your wisdom to guide me to that place of perfect peace and joy, which is my Maximized Life. In Jesus' name, Amen.

Maximizing Moments:
Life is about choices. Will you choose today to be a Maximizer? Will you choose today to confront your problems no matter what they are with the confidence that God has a plan to turn them around?

Maximizing Mantra:
I am anointed to solve problems!

DAY 5 – MORE CHOICES THAT MATTER

*"Oh, that you would choose life,
so that you and your descendants might live!"*
Deuteronomy 30:19 (NLT)

Problems are about you! They are about the decisions you make and the actions you take in response to them. You learned yesterday to refocus, to remember, and to rehearse.

The state of your mind is crucial in problem solving and planning. We are taught by the Bible to *"be transformed (changed) by the [entire] renewal of your mind [by its new ideals and its new attitude]"* (Romans 12:2 AMP). The choices that you are called to make are intelligent, faith inspired, and well-reasoned. The battlefield of your mind needs to be actively engaged with a determination to win. The way you win the battles in your mind is to renew it through a new thought process.

The Bible is the source of Truth to which your mind must be renewed. As you continue to talk about choices, you are being called upon to elevate your thinking to a higher level.

Today there are some more quality choices that you must make:

Choose to research. Answers are all around you! As you learned a couple of days ago, whatever you are facing is not unique to you! Your answer is somewhere! Because you are not going to allow your emotions to rule over you during problem solving, you should put your mind to work. Start looking for others who have faced a problem similar to yours and investigate how they persevered. Your research should start with Scripture. Is there a biblical person who faced something similar to you? If so, what did they do? How did they do it? You must remember that God teaches you through precept and example. You can learn from biblical examples. Once

Reality of Problems

you have exhausted your biblical search, you should look for contemporary people who have solved similar problems. The Internet makes this search much easier. Never be tricked into thinking that you are the only one facing your problem. Books are also another source of research. Take the time to research all your options.

Choose to respond. Never react but respond! What's the difference? It is more than a play on words. Reaction is motivated by emotion. Responding is motivated by deliberate calculation. When one reacts, there is an emotionally charged action. One who is on the Maximized Life Journey responds to problems with targeted focus. That's the difference! You should choose to be a responder, not a reactor. Problems can push a lot of buttons in your life; and if you react in kind, you will exacerbate the problem, not resolve it. Responders seek resolution. Think back on times when you have been pushed to react. It was emotional and impulsive. More often than not, these behaviors led to regrets. When you take the time to respond, you are calculating how to manage and solve the problem. Don't be ruled by your emotions because they will derail your problem solving. Respond appropriately by choosing to act in faith, not fear.

Choose to rely. Can you recall a time when you were encouraged to trust God? As hopeful as these words sounded, without understanding how to trust God, the comfort of these words soon wore off. If you are going to fulfill this journey, you will need to decide to trust God. To trust God means to walk by faith. (You will learn about faith on Days 9 through 15). You must choose to believe God's report on your situation: *"Trust in the Lord with all your heart; do not depend on your own understanding. Seek His will in* *all you do, and he will show you which path to take. Don't be impressed with your own wisdom"* (Proverbs 3:5-7a NLT).

Relying on God is much simpler than you may have thought. It is about standing on God's Word and not standing on our own wisdom. As you rehearse God's Word, you must resolve to act like His Word is Truth. Regardless of what you see, God's Word is true. God's Word will change any problem you face. If you will stand on God's Word, you will see every problem brought to successful completion and God will be glorified.

The last choice that you must make is purely an act of faith! When the Maximized Life appears, you will be more than ready to glorify God. However, as you are on this journey, can you praise God?

Choose to rejoice. The choice to praise God before you can see the results is affirmed in Scripture. King David faced problems and made up his mind to sing praises to God—all based upon God's promises and proven faithfulness. David declared, *"Therefore I will offer sacrifices of joy in His tabernacle; I will sing, yes, I will sing praises to the LORD"* (Psalm 27:6b NKJ). In the face of besetting enemies, David declared God's promises and relied upon His faithfulness. Through the tears and trouble, David rejoiced! For the last couple of days, you have been on this journey. With the mountains before you and enemies behind you, can you rejoice? To *rejoice* means to "cause joy." This is devoid of feelings. Can you cause yourself to joy while you are on this Journey?

Take some time today, and every day, to rejoice! Be thankful to God for His presence and promises. Rejoice in the fact that when your problems are settled, you will be promoted. That's worth rejoicing.

Reality of Problems

All of these choices will lead to life—not just for you but for your children and children's children, too. Now this is a Maximized Life!

Maximized Prayer:
Father, I choose Your way, which is life and that more abundantly! I rejoice in your faithfulness to me as Your child. In Jesus' name, Amen.

Maximizing Moments:
There is more at stake than just you. Write out all the people and relationships that are affected by your life and who will be blessed because you chose to Maximize Your Life.

Write down the answers to the following questions:
- What problems are you facing?
- What biblical person handled a similar problem?
- Who do you know personally who had a similar problem and what did they do to address their problem?

Maximizing Mantra:
I give thanks in everything, for God is on my side!

DAY 6 – THE POWER OF PARTNERSHIPS

*"Two people are better off than one,
for they can help each other succeed."*
Ecclesiastes 4:9 (NLT)

Developing a partnership mentality is paramount to your Maximize Life Journey. When you value and respect partnerships, your journey will become easier and you will not feel alone.

Partnership is a revolutionary approach to accelerated success in life. It is a thread that runs through the entire fabric of your existence: *"Two people are better than one, because they get more done by working together. If one falls down, the other can help him up. But it is bad for the person who is alone and falls, because no one is there to help. If two lie down together, they will be warm, but a person alone will not be warm. An enemy might defeat one person, but two people together can defend themselves; a rope that is woven of three strings is hard to break"* (Ecclesiastes 4:9-12 NCV). In other words, everyone needs someone.

It appears that whatever God gives a person to do, He never expects it to be completed alone! When Moses received instructions from God to serve as a deliverer for Israel, Moses was concerned about his speech. God provided him a partner in Aaron. When Moses was in the wilderness without a GPS, he partnered with Hobab for his navigation ability. When Nehemiah was going to rebuild the wall of Jerusalem, he partnered with King Artaxerxes, who opened up doors of opportunity for him so that he could get all the materials he needed for his task. Nehemiah also partnered with the people to accomplish this great and monumental task. Without the king and people's partnership, Nehemiah would not have been as successful. One of the very first things that Jesus did in his earthly ministry was to find 12 men to partner with Him. You read of their

Respect for Partnerships

role throughout the Gospels. Jesus' mission was furthered because He had partners.

You cannot underestimate the importance of the disciples to Jesus' ministry. You may ask why? Well, if Jesus had not invested in partners before His arrest, death, and ascension into Heaven, the salvation message would not have had competent people to deliver it. The death of Jesus would have been just another historic event rather than the regeneration of a people. WOW!!! See how important partnerships are when they are taken seriously. These disciples took Jesus' last command and made it their first concern: *"Go ye therefore, and teach all nations, baptizing them in the name of the Father, and of the Son, and of the Holy Ghost: Teaching them to observe all things whatsoever I have commanded you: and, lo, I am with you always, even unto the end of the world. Amen"* (Matthew 28:19-20 KJV). Had the disciples taken His words lightly and said, "Well, He is going away; we don't have to do what He says," we may never have heard of the wonderful saving power of Jesus Christ. Committed partners will give you the necessary assistance for your Journey.

Another example of the power of partnerships is seen with the Apostle Paul. He had several partnerships, but they all had different purposes. He partnered with many people as he traveled to spread the Gospel. He could not have done it alone. Paul partnered with the entire Church of Philippi. This church served as a financial partner for Paul's ministry. They sent monetary gifts to him so that he could continue to travel and preach the Gospel. In fact, He said, *"It was good of you to help me when I was having such a hard time. My friends at Philippi, you remember what it was like when I started preaching the good news in Macedonia. After I left there, you were the*

Day 6 – The Power of Partnerships

only church that became my partner by giving blessings and by receiving them in return. Even when I was in Thessalonica, you helped me more than once" (Philippians 4:14-16 CEV). Paul placed a high value on the partners that help him succeed.

Partnership is a state of relationship between two or more individuals who have a conscious, calculated, and consistent commitment to each other based on unshakeable convictions to a common cause.

Partnership is a God concept that is evidenced from the beginning of creation. You were created to be in partnership with God from the very beginning. When God created you, He designed you to be His representative in the earth, to bring about His will: *"Then God said, 'Let Us make man in Our image, according to Our likeness; let them have dominion over the fish of the sea, over the birds of the air, and over the cattle, over all the earth and over every creeping thing that creeps on the earth'"* (Genesis 1:26 KJV). When God said, *"Let us,"* He was partnering with the Holy Spirit and His Son. We were formed out of a divine partnership; this means we have the innate ability to form partnerships with God and others. And, as we learned on Day 2, we are not fulfilled unless we are in partnership with God and others.

There are many different kinds of partnerships that we have in life. There are *Congenial Partnerships*. These are partnerships that are born out of family ties. (These are marital, familial or parental relationships.) When properly leveraged, these partnerships can bring added effectiveness to your life. Whether it is with your spouse or children, you will need congenial partners. Then, there are *Covenant Partnerships*. These are partnerships that are based on

Respect for Partnerships

contractual agreements. These may be verbal or written agreements, but there is a clearly defined covenant that drives the partnership.

Also, there are *Casual Partnerships*. These are usually temporary in nature. For example, if you ask a neighbor to help you move some furniture in your backyard, you are partnering with this project. However, this partnership ends as soon as the furniture is moved.

You will find that you have *Commercial Partnerships*. These partnerships are mainly in the business arena. They may be legal or informal, but they help advance economic interests. As a Believer, you engage in *Christian Partnerships*. These partnerships are related to advancing God's work on the earth. The Gospel is so important that God uses teams to carry it!

Coaching Partnerships will aid your development process. These are partnerships that are based around a mentor/protégée relationship. You will grow to the degree that you allow others to have positive input into your life.

There is significant power in partnerships! The first partner is God! After that, you will have many different types of partnerships with people. These are all key to your Maximized Life Journey! Embrace partnership today as God's way to assist you in reaching your destination more quickly. Two people are better than one!

Day 6 - The Power of Partnerships

Maximized Prayer:
>Father, help me to see those whom You have planted around me who are destined to help me maximize my life!
>Help me to respect these relationships and never squander them. In Jesus' name, Amen.

Maximizing Moments:
>What are the key partnerships that you need to help solve your most urgent problems? Identify people who will fill these roles.
>
>In what ways can you make a greater contribution to the partnerships in your life?

Maximizing Mantra:
>I work together with God and others to maximize my life!

NOTES

DAY 7 – PARTNERING WITH EXCELLENCE

"And whatsoever ye do, do it heartily, as to the Lord, and not unto men; Knowing that of the Lord ye shall receive the reward of the inheritance: for ye serve the Lord Christ."
Colossians 3:23-24 (KJV)

Today starts with a caution. Because there is a level of interconnectedness that exists between you and your partners (other people), it is important to know that most people in life are takers. They are only concerned about what they can get out of a relationship. You must be very careful about the people with whom you partner because if their intention is to use you, that partnership will hinder your journey!

Partnerships must be mutually beneficial. Partners must be givers. They must give of themselves, their service, and their substance. Because partnerships are birthed out of a calculated commitment, you should examine every potential partnership for its alignment with your purpose. What will anchor your partnership is the cause (purpose). You must have an unshakeable understanding that whatever you give to the partnership, God will honor it; and it will reap benefits in your life (Ephesians 6:8).

With all this in mind, how should you manage your partnerships? (How you manage these earthly partnerships is what qualifies you to partner with God for something big!) True riches come from partnerships well managed!

You handle your partnership through a *Stewardship Consciousness*. This means clearly understanding what your role is in the partnership and fulfilling it with excellence. Excellence pays attention to detail and gives birth to superior performance, which causes maximized potential and promotion in life and brings glory to God. To be a partner of excellence, you cannot contribute the

Respect for Partnerships

average or the minimum. You must go the extra mile to accomplish any goal. The way that you manage your partnerships will determine what you get from the partnership.

The *Strength of Commitment* to the partnership will determine what your partnership can accomplish and the benefit it will be to your life. Ask yourself, "Is the partnership stronger because of my presence or am I just a liability? Do I always have excuses why I can't fulfill my obligations to the partnership or does my commitment rise to the occasion?" Excuses are like weeds; they grow uncultivated. Excuses are lies wrapped up in reasons. You must possess the strength of character to stay committed to the partnership. If you remove all excuses and remain committed to the partnership, there are no limits as to where that alliance will take you.

The next way you respect partnerships is by *Spiritual Convictions*. The Bible says, *"Let each man be fully convinced in his own mind"* (Romans 14:5 NKJ). Your spiritual convictions will be a great barometer for how you manage your partnerships. They will also guard you against the proposal of indecent partnerships. Integrity and spiritual principles must govern your partnerships so that they do not become perverted!

Partnerships are successfully built when there is faithfulness from both parties: *"If you are faithful in little things, you will be faithful in large ones. But if you are dishonest in little things, you won't be honest with greater responsibilities . . . And if you are not faithful with other people's things, why should you be trusted with things of your own?"* (Luke 16:10, 12 NLT). This is a powerful passage on promotion. You will be promoted based upon how you manage the partnerships that God has placed in your life. Your promotion hinges on your ongoing respect and investment in your partnerships. When

Day 7 - Respecting Partnerships

faithfulness has been established, there is a level of commitment that transcends the average: *"Knowing that whatsoever good thing any man doeth, the same shall he receive of the Lord, whether he be bond or free"* (Ephesians 6:8 KJV).

When you choose a partner, you should look for someone who can get the job done. Partners bring a perspective to the table that you do not have. So don't get intimidated when people don't think like you. The reason is because you are not always right: *"Plans go wrong for lack of advice; many advisers bring success"* (Proverbs 15:22 NLT). An advisor partners with you to give you wise counsel. Well, then, that means you could read Proverbs 15:22 this way: *"Plans go wrong for lack of partners; many partners bring success."* So, when you look at it this way, you are looking for partners to help you Maximize Your Life: *"Where no wise guidance is, the people fall, but in the multitude of counselors there is safety"* (Proverbs 11:14 AMP). You can do the same thing in this Scripture and read it this way: *"Where no wise guidance is, the people fall, but in the multitude of partners there is safety."* When you are connected to people who are anchored in the same cause as you, you will find safety. People who are real partners with you will not want to see you fail or even live a mediocre life. They are active participants in your destiny.

A mutually beneficial partnership means everyone in the partnership is doing his or her part to its maximum potential. Your participation in this partnership needs to reflect that you know and recognize that others are counting on you. In the same way that you do not want to be joined in a partnership with someone who is user, you do not want to be a user either!

When you grasp the partnership principle, you will begin to treasure the meaning of partnership and the people who God brings

Respect for Partnerships

into your life. You will soon see that God is orchestrating partnerships to advance you on your journey! Honor these partnerships because they are a gift from God! God uses partnerships throughout the Bible and He uses them today. Allow your partnerships to bring glory to God! You will be able to accomplish everything that God has given you to do—and more!

Maximized Prayer:

Father, I respect all the partnerships you have brought into my life! I vow to handle them with honor and respect so that You get the glory. In Jesus' name, Amen.

Maximizing Moments:

What behaviors have you engaged in that jeopardized the partnerships that God has put into your life?

How can you raise the level of your commitment to the family partnership?

Maximizing Mantra:

God brings me into the company of the people I need to know.

Day 8 – Maximizing Partnerships

*"I promise that when any two of you on earth
agree about something you are praying for,
my Father in heaven will do it for you."*
Matthew 18:19 (CEV)

Once you have gained a respect for your partnerships, you should turn your attention to how to get the most from them. In order for this to happen, it will require that you change! Change is not bad! So there is no need to fear. Change is designed to bring you out of your comfort zone into a place where you can maximize your potential. Change is the purposeful effort that is sustained and assisted by divine help. It is your responsibility to bring yourself to a place of change. Change is a product of human effort sustained by divine help.

Change requires honesty and knowledge. Change occurs on purpose and it is by design. When truth is embraced, change must take place. There is no way that you can remain the same when you come to the understanding of something that needs to change. A commitment to change requires more than exposure to information and logical reasoning. Change requires discipline, which means enforced obedience. It is not by chance but by design.

In order to Maximize Your Life, you must begin new behaviors as they relate to your partnerships so that you can get the most from those divine connections. One sure way to anchor a change in behavior is the resolve of repetition. Repetition enforces change. The more you do something, the easier it becomes. Sometimes the changes are the types of people with whom you partner, the types of places you frequent, or the types of things you do in the partnership. Thank God that you are not alone in the partnership process. God will help you by brining you into the company of the people you need to know who are crucial to your Maximized Life! The right partners are there waiting for you, and you are important to each other's journey. God will orchestrate this if you maximize your partnership with Him.

When Abram (Abraham) understood that he was partnering with God, he had to make some changes, also. These changes accelerated his success and increased his prosperity. Take a look at the changes Abram made to maximize his life through partnership with God: *"After Lot separated from him, GOD said to Abram, 'Open your eyes, look around. Look north, south, east, and west. Everything you see, the whole land spread out before you, I will give to you and your children forever. I'll make your descendants like dust—counting your descendants will be as impossible as counting the dust of the Earth. So—on your feet, get moving! Walk through the country, its length and breadth; I'm giving it all to you.' Abram moved his tent. He went and settled by the Oaks of Mamre in Hebron. There he built an altar to GOD"* (Genesis 13:14-17 MSG).

There are three changes that Abram made. First, he changed his perspective. He was instructed to *"open his eyes."* God was stretching his capacity to believe and to receive. God gave Abram a strategy, which would open him up to new possibilities. This is what good partners do! They do not allow you to stay the way you are. They motivate and challenge you to excel in life. Abram had to view things differently and know that God was his chief partner. No matter what Abram had given up, sacrificed, or left for the sake of this partnership, God would replace beyond his wildest dreams. This is why your number one partnership needs to be with God. His promise to you is that He will be with you and tell you "*marvelous*

Day 8 - Maximizing Partnerships

and wondrous things that you could never figure out on your own" (Jeremiah 33:3 MSG).

Next, Abram changed his position. At God's direction, Abram moved from familiar places and people to a place of God's choosing. Complacency and stagnation are enemies to progress. When Abram changed his position, he repositioned himself to hear from God and receive all that God had destined for Him (The Maximized Life). Abram's obedience to change positions, even before he saw all that God had promised, served as a prequalifier. Abram demonstrated to God that he could be trusted and that he was going to take the partnership with God seriously. After Abram separated from Lot, *then* God spoke of all the glorious plans He had for Abram.

What makes this very interesting is that God did not speak to him concerning the partnership and benefits until this separation had taken place. Perhaps you have been abandoned or you feel that someone left you prematurely. Can it be that God is repositioning you to receive a greater blessing? Sometimes progress cannot be made in your life until people barriers are removed. There may be people on your current journey who cannot handle where you are going. Their presence in your life will serve as a distraction or delay. This Maximized Life Journey will cause you to gain a new perspective on the people in your life, and then you will have to reposition yourself. Can the people around you handle where you are going? Some people in your life are accustomed to seeing you struggle and be unhappy. What happens when you are living the Maximized Life? Rather than allowing them to hold you back, you may need to change your position by redefining the relationships. Then, once you have arrived at your destination, build bridges for them to follow!

Respect for Partnerships

Last, Abram changed his praise. Abram regularly acknowledged his Chief Partner! He did this through establishing altars where he worshipped God. Altars are an important aspect of the Believer's life because they remind us of our dependence on someone other than ourselves! Altars also remind us to stop and thank God! Abram knew that his life was directed by God's hand. Your Maximized Life Journey will never be successful without the active assistance of God! And you should praise Him for this! A Maximizer acknowledges God's preeminence and His partnership! (Later in this journey, you will learn how to offer effective praise to God.)

When you partner with God to advance His Kingdom, He will take care of you—very well. Look at this passage from Scripture: *"That night God appeared to Solomon. God said, 'What do you want from me? Ask.' Solomon answered, 'You were extravagantly generous with David my father, and now you have made me king in his place. Establish, GOD, the words you spoke to my father, for you've given me a staggering task, ruling this mob of people. Yes, give me wisdom and knowledge as I come and go among this people—for who on his own is capable of leading these, your glorious people.' God answered Solomon, 'This is what has come out of your heart: You didn't grasp for money, wealth, fame, and the doom of your enemies; you didn't even ask for a long life. You asked for wisdom and knowledge so you could govern well my people over whom I've made you king. Because of this, you get what you asked for—wisdom and knowledge. And I'm presenting you the rest as a bonus—money, wealth, and fame beyond anything the kings before or after you had or will have'"* (2 Chronicles 1:7-11 MSG). When you put purpose—God's purposes for your life—as a priority, God will honor you: "When what is important to God, becomes important to you, then what is important to you becomes important to God."

Day 8 - Maximizing Partnerships

Your Maximized Life is not just about your financial and material advancement. It's about living your purpose. Most people do not understand this and so they reach for things—cars, houses, positions, and possessions. However, in God's system, He will provide for you as you pursue purpose! This keeps the Maximizer from becoming a user or parasite. You should never use people to get things. This is a perversion of the partnership principle. God places people in your life to better you as a person. As you become a better person and align with God's plans and principles, then you will walk in His abundance. (The Maximized Life Journey is God's tool to assist you in this developmental process.)

Start today maximizing your relationship with God! He will enable you to maximize your relationships with others. God wants to help you in this journey! Let Him! Rely upon Him daily to guide you and you will end this 52-day journey with victory!

Maximized Prayer:
Father, I repent for mishandling my partnership with You! I have not relied upon You as I should. I correct that today. In Jesus' name, Amen.

Maximizing Moments:
What role have you allowed God to play in your life?

What are the ways that you can enhance your relationship with Him?

Maximizing Mantra:
God is my Chief Partner and I maximize my relationship with Him!

Respect for Partnerships

NOTES

DAY 9 – IT STARTS WITH YOUR FAITH

"Faith is the confidence that what we hope for will actually happen; it gives us assurance about things we cannot see."
Hebrews 11:1 (KJV)

You are making good progress on the journey. Take a moment now to thank God for what you are learning. For the next couple of days, you will learn how to use the resources that God has put at your disposal! A Maximizer uses all resources that are available. Most people are unaware that God is so vested in their success that He has given them the tools to their success. You will discover these as you continue on your journey this week.

The key resourcefulness principle God has made available to you is faith! Learning to operate in faith is the key to your Maximized Life. Faith is not a foreign word to Believers. But what it really means and how to operate in it usually are! Most people know they need faith but are not certain how to get it (or, if they even have it, how to use it). And, because of this, many Christians miss a vital part of their walk with God.

Let's see what the Bible says about faith and your life:

"And my righteous ones will live by faith. But I will take no pleasure in anyone who turns away." (Hebrews 10:38 NLT)

"And Jesus answering saith unto them, 'Have faith in God.'" (Mark 11:22 KJV)

"And He said to her, 'Daughter, be of good cheer; your faith has made you well. Go in peace.'" (Luke 8:48 KJV)

"But if God so clothes the grass, which is alive in the field today, and tomorrow is thrown into the oven, how much more will he clothe you, O you of little faith!" (Luke 12:28 ESV)

Resourcefulness Principles

"The apostles said to the Lord, 'Show us how to increase our faith.'" (Luke 17:5 NLT)

"And it is impossible to please God without faith." (Hebrews 11:6 NLT)

From this very small representation of Scriptures, it is evident that faith should play an active role in the life of the Christian. You were designed to live by faith! Everything you need God to do in your life can be acquired through faith: healing, peace, love, and provisions. Prior to today's reading, you may have felt that you were "in faith." In some areas, you very well may be; but in others, you may not be!

Let's take a moment and perform a faith checkup. *"But Christ has rescued us from the curse pronounced by the law. When he was hung on the cross, he took upon himself the curse for our wrongdoing. For it is written in the Scriptures, 'Cursed is everyone who is hung on a tree.' Through Christ Jesus, God has blessed the Gentiles with the same blessing he promised to Abraham, so that we who are Believers might receive the promised Holy Spirit through faith"* (Galatians 3:13-14 NLT). The redemptive power of God, which was demonstrated on the cross, redeemed humanity from living by the dictates of human ability and activity. And, as a result, Christians can receive the promised Holy Spirit *by faith*! Though this verse references a specific promise—receiving the Holy Spirit—faith is a universal principle that applies to every area of your life. Every principle and promise from Scripture is received by faith. Learning to operate in faith is critical to the Maximized Life Journey.

Here is a simple test to see whether or not you are maximizing the faith process:

Day 9 - It Starts with Your Faith

- First, do you listen to, on average, at least 1 hour of the Word daily? (Faith comes by hearing. Maximizers intentionally saturate themselves with the Word of God.)
- Second, do you speak God's Word over your life daily? (According to Mark 11:23, faith is released by the words of your mouth. Maximizers discipline themselves to speak God's Word over the circumstances in life.)
- Third, do you act in agreement with what you prayed and believed? (Corresponding action is critical to experience faith results).

If you answered no to any of these questions, it means you need a faith booster! Walking and living by faith is not difficult, but most people do not understand how to do it—or they don't do it consistently. In either case, limited results are seen. As a Maximizer, you will never settle for limited results! You want to get everything that God has in store for you!

So what is faith? Faith is the supernatural power of God made available to you so that you can transform conditions, circumstances, and situations based upon the will of God. When you operate in faith, God respects it, rewards it, and responds to it. So where do you find out about this supernatural power of God called Faith? You guessed it, in the Bible: *"And Jesus answered them, 'Have faith in God. Truly, I say to you, whoever says to this mountain, "Be taken up and thrown into the sea," and does not doubt in his heart, but believes that what he says will come to pass, it will be done for him. Therefore I tell you, whatever you ask in prayer, believe that you have received it, and it will be yours. And whenever you stand praying, forgive, if you have anything against anyone, so that your Father also who is in heaven may forgive you your trespasses'"* (Mark 11:22-25 NLT). In

Resourcefulness Principles

these verses are the foundation of faith. When you learn this, you will be able to operate at a whole new level!

Faith can only be released where the will of God is known (Romans 10:17). God's will is known from the Bible—and the Bible only! Faith is not positive thinking. It is a supernatural power to change anything! You can only have what you believe you receive at the moment you pray. God needs your permission and your participation to get involved in your life and situation. Operating by faith gives God the permission to act for you! Conversely, fear will tie God's hands and restrict Him from working for you!

Boldness in faith is born out of trust that you have in God's faithfulness! During times of challenge, the devil approaches you and attempts to steal your faith—that will happen during this journey; you must not allow it! When you choose to live by faith, you will never operate solely based on your abilities or limitations but on God's promises! Faith is vital to completing your Maximized Life Journey.

Tomorrow you will learn the eight (8) steps to using your faith.

Day 9 - It Starts with Your Faith

Maximized Prayer:
> Father, I accept the force of faith that You have made available to me! I want to please You; therefore, I decide today to walk by faith and not by my feelings. In Jesus' name, Amen.

Maximizing Moments:
> Are there areas of your life where you are afraid? List them.
>
> Can you find Scriptures where God has made a promise to you concerning these areas? (Visit the maximizedlifejourney.com website and search there.)
>
> Develop a habit of listening to the Word of God being taught daily. Will you commit to this?

Maximizing Mantra:
> I please God because I operate by faith!

NOTES

DAY 10 – IT'S ALRIGHT TO ASK

*"'You don't have enough faith,' Jesus told them. ' I tell you the truth,
if you had faith even as small as a mustard seed,
you could say to this mountain, "Move from here to there,"
and it would move. Nothing would be impossible.'"*
Matthew 17:20 (NLT)

Yesterday you learned that faith is a systematic spiritual process that you use to access the promises of God. Because faith is a process, the results will be progressive; you may not see them all at once, but there will always be results! If you will respect the process that you will learn over the next couple of days, you will eliminate the frustration that most Christians have. When it comes to living by faith, you do not need to know how faith works; if you will just understand the process and how to make it work in your life, it will always work!

Maximizers are results-oriented and you will experience them progressively. Early on, the results may be small. But there will always be results from the faith process. So, to maximize the system, you must learn the laws (components) of the system.

One of the greatest examples of faith can be found in the life of Abraham: *"We call Abraham 'father' not because he got God's attention by living like a saint, but because God made something out of Abraham when he was a nobody. Isn't that what we've always read in Scripture, God saying to Abraham, 'I set you up as father of many peoples'? Abraham was first named 'father' and then became a father because he dared to trust God to do what only God could do: raise the dead to life, with a word make something out of nothing. When everything was hopeless, Abraham believed anyway, deciding to live not on the basis of what he saw he couldn't do but on what God said he would do. And so he was made father of a multitude of peoples. God himself said to him,*

Resourcefulness Principles

'You're going to have a big family, Abraham!' Abraham didn't focus on his own impotence and say, 'It's hopeless. This hundred-year-old body could never father a child.' Nor did he survey Sarah's decades of infertility and give up. He didn't tiptoe around God's promise asking cautiously skeptical questions. He plunged into the promise and came up strong, ready for God, sure that God would make good on what he had said. That's why it is said, 'Abraham was declared fit before God by trusting God to set him right'" (Romans 4:17-20 MSG).

As you can see, Abraham faced an impossible situation. Yet his faith produced the results God had promised. Abraham worked the faith process and received results. He waited for 25 years, and each year it seemed more and more impossible. Yet his faith was working! All the odds were against Sarah and him. Yet they believed God. Although God wanted to bless Abraham, God could not bless Abraham beyond his faith! So God taught Abraham how to operate in faith. Each of the components of this system can be seen in Abraham's life, and he is now called the "Father of the Faith."

There is so much that God has in store for you! You cannot even conceive of all that He has for you: *"God can do anything, you know—far more than you could ever imagine or guess or request in your wildest dreams! He does it not by pushing us around but by working within us"* (Ephesians 3:20 MSG). If Abraham could wait 25 years with discipline, you can certainly wait a few days. This is a faith process, not magic! Faith is not a "get rich quick" scheme. It is a disciplined lifestyle, which gives you the ability to tap into the creative power of God, which will change circumstances, situations, and conditions over which you have been given authority.

Now it's time for you to learn it as well. The first component of the faith process is "asking"—making a petition. A petition is a

Day 10 - It's Alright to Ask

sincere, earnest request made by one expecting to receive. Here is what Jesus taught about prayer: *"Ask, and you will receive. Search, and you will find. Knock, and the door will be opened for you"* (Matthew 7:7 CEV). You should not be embarrassed to ask God for anything. You should be convinced that God allows you to ask! Jabez asked and God granted his request (1 Chronicles 4:10). Two of Jesus' disciples approached Him one day and asked Him what appeared to be an outrageous question. Yet Jesus did not reprimand them for asking! He reminded them that their request was not within his authority to grant (Mark 10:35-40). Hannah asked for children and God granted her request (1 Samuel 1:9-17). You should feel free to ask God for what you need—and want!

God has let you know what He wants you to have. He gave you parameters. You cannot ask for anything that will violate His laws or His nature (2 Peter 1:3; 1 Timothy 6:17). However, God does want your joy to be full! You can ask for anything that pertains to your life: *"This is what I want you to do: Ask the Father for whatever is in keeping with the things I've revealed to you. Ask in my name, according to my will, and he'll most certainly give it to you. Your joy will be a river overflowing its banks"* (John 16:24 MSG)! You can ask for anything that is promised to you in the Bible. There is peace in the Bible, so you can ask for it. There is freedom from fear in the Bible; therefore, you can ask for a fear-free life. Joy is in the Bible, and you can ask for your joy to be restored!

As Jesus instructed His disciples, you should ask the Father in Jesus' name. All prayer should be addressed to God the Father. When you ask, you should ask according to God's revealed will. And you know that God's will is found in His Word! You will have a confidence when you know that you are asking for something that

Resourcefulness Principles

lines up with God's promises: *"And this is the confidence that we have in him, that, if we ask any thing according to his will, he heareth us: And if we know that he hear us, whatsoever we ask, we know that we have the petitions that we desired of him"* (1 John 5:14-15 KJV).

Once your request is located in the Word of God, you should ask in faith without wavering. Wavering represents doubt and fear. You have already seen that when God makes a promise, He dispatches His power to fulfill it! God will not fail you! According to Mark 4:26, at this stage of the faith process, it is doubtful that you will know how God will bring your petition to pass. It is extremely important that you be confident that He is both able and willing to perform His word. If you really believe that God hears you, then you should have the confidence that you have the petitions that you have asked from Him: *"So I tell you to believe that you have received the things you ask for in prayer, and God will give them to you"* (Mark 11:24 NCV).

When you finish your prayer time, it may not feel like anything is different. However, you must divorce yourself from feelings. Feelings are an emotional response; and, usually, they are the result of the senses (sight, sound, smell, taste, touch). You as a Maximizer do not walk by sight (senses) but by faith! Once you pray in faith, you must work the rest of the faith process with discipline.

Day 10 - It's Alright to Ask

Maximized Prayer:
Father, you delight to give me the desires of my heart. I take the limits off of you! I cannot deplete you by asking you for what I need. I receive everything that you have established for me that pertains to life and godliness. In Jesus' name, Amen.

Maximizing Moments:
What are the areas in your life that need maximizing? (Be specific.)

Relate all these needs to scriptural promises and craft a prayer that affirms these promises.

Maximizing Mantra:
I have faith!

NOTES

DAY 11 – LEARNING TO BELIEVE

*"What do you mean, 'If I can'? Jesus asked.
'Anything is possible if a person believes.'"*
Mark 9:23 (NLT)

What you are able to believe establishes what is possible for you! What you are about to learn today will revolutionize how you think from this day forward. The possibilities for your life will never be determined by what others have done or are doing. Possibilities for the Maximizer will be established by what you are able to believe. The more you expand your capacity to believe, the greater the possibilities for your life! The only one who can keep you from the awesome possibilities that God has designed for you is you!

The development of your faith will expand your possibilities. Based upon the Scripture reading today, anything is possible for you if you believe. Believing not only sets the boundaries for your life, it also forms the basis of your faith. Your faith cannot work if you do not believe! Yesterday you saw that prayer is effective only to the degree that you *"believe you receive when you pray"* (Mark 11:24 KJV). Believing that it will happen sometime in the future is not faith.

Your ability to believe is based upon pre-established criteria. Throughout your life, you have been gathering information about possibilities and what you are willing to believe. Each person—you included—has set criteria to determine what he or she will believe. Believing is an act of your will! You must will to believe beyond the norm.

After Jesus was raised from the dead, He appeared to most of His disciples. However, Thomas was not there. He missed one of the most historically significant events of all time—the Resurrection

Resourcefulness Principles

of Jesus! When the other disciples tried to convince him of what they had seen, Thomas refused to believe unless his criteria were met: *"The other disciples therefore said to him, 'We have seen the Lord.' So he said to them, 'Unless I see in His hands the print of the nails, and put my finger into the print of the nails, and put my hand into His side, I will not believe'"* (John 20:25 NKJ). Like Thomas, you are in control of your belief system; you will allow yourself to believe or disbelieve information. You determine if something is factual (believable or not).

Thomas required sense realm (information provided by the senses) evidence before he would believe. On this journey, you will need to elevate your belief structure beyond what your senses will provide. A new criterion is required for the Maximizer! When Jesus approached Thomas, He revealed to him another level of believing: *"Jesus said, 'So, you believe because you've seen with your own eyes. Even better blessings are in store for those who believe without seeing'"* (John 20:29 MSG). Rather than waiting to believe after one has seen, Jesus says that there is a higher way of operating—believing before seeing.

Biblical believing is to accept something as a fact without having any sense realm evidence. To be sure, it does not mean that you don't need any evidence, just not sense realm evidence. The most significant evidence to the Believer is God's Word.

God's Word lets us know that there is an entire world that we cannot see with our natural eyes: *"For by him were all things created, that are in heaven, and that are in earth, visible and invisible, whether they be thrones, or dominions, or principalities, or powers: all things were created by him, and for him"* (Colossians 1:16 KJV). There is an invisible (not seen by human eyes) world created by God. We can grasp that God is invisible and heaven is invisible, but there are also other invisible things in that realm. We should pay attention to the invisible world (spirit realm) more than the visible world (natural realm). In fact, the invisible world is more real than the visible world. To fully grasp this, we must have a major paradigm shift in our thinking. Most people were taught that seeing is believing! However, from God's perspective, the things that you see are not as reliable as the things that you cannot see (invisible world): *"As we look not to the things that are seen but to the things that are unseen. For the things that are seen are transient, but the things that are unseen are eternal"* (2 Corinthians 4:18 ESV).

This invisible world is preexistent to the visible world and it is eternal. In fact, all the things that exist today were created from spirit realm things which you cannot see: *"Because of our faith, we know that the world was made at God's command. We also know that what can be seen was made out of what cannot be seen"* (Hebrews 11:3 CEV). God's Word framed everything! And His Word still has power to frame your world! The evidence that you have of this unseen world is the Word of God, or your faith: *"Faith is the confidence that what we hope for will actually happen; it gives us assurance about things we cannot see"* (Hebrews 11:1 NLT).

God impacts the natural world from the spiritual world. Everything you will ever need is already in existence in the spiritual world (Ephesians 1:3). It is just in a spiritual raw material state. Knowing this means that it should be easier to believe for what we cannot see (naturally) since what we see is created from what we cannot see (spiritually). The things for which you ask, though you cannot see them, are in a raw, invisible state. The faith that you possess enables you to make a supernatural transfer from the

Resourcefulness Principles

invisible world to the visible world. When you ask God for something, He already knows that you need it and has already made provision for it in that unseen world. Try seeing things from God's perspective. You must start seeing beyond what you can see with your natural eyes!

You may be seeing financial lack in all of your bank accounts. However, from God's perspective, your every need is already met in abundance; this is a spirit realm fact. From God's perspective, what belongs to you in the spirit world is just as much your possession as what you have in the natural world. Biblical believing is seeing situations and circumstances from God's perspective. You are not in denial when you speak God's promises over your life! You're in faith! You are seeing it from a different perspective. You have heard people say that the glass is half full or half empty. The different views are based on perspective. Your capacity to see things from God's perspective is shaped by how you were raised, the people who formed your belief system, repetitious information to which you have been exposed, and experiences that you have had. (Later in the journey, you will learn more about this.)

Your mind must be conditioned to approach situations like God! So, when God made a promise to Abram (Abraham), Abram was incapable of seeing the enormity of what God was promising. God took him outside and showed him sand on the shore and the stars in the sky and helped him associate the promise of multitudes with the stars in the sky (Genesis 15:4-6). From that point, every time Abram looked up at the stars or down at the sand, he saw a multitude of children! Abram's capacity to believe expanded and it came to pass! The same will be true for you!

Day 11 - Learning to Believe

Start today relying on that invisible world to help you. Start seeing things from God's perspective. God has already seen your future and it looks great!

Maximized Prayer:
>Father, I marvel at how orderly You are. You created everything by Your Word. I rely on Your Word to transform my life and bring order. In Jesus' name, Amen.

Maximizing Moments:
>Begin to see your life from God's perspective. He does not see you lacking anything. Look at every area of your life and begin to speak God's perspective on those situations.

Maximizing Mantra:
>I am not moved by what I see or what I feel; I am moved by what I believe!

Notes

Day 12 – Words and Works

"I tell you the truth, you can say to this mountain, 'May you be lifted up and thrown into the sea,' and it will happen. But you must really believe it will happen and have no doubt in your heart."
Mark 11:23 (NLT)

Your words matter! You cannot hear this enough! The Bible calls this confession. A faith confession is a statement you choose to make in agreement with God's Word regardless of your situation. Regardless of how your life looks, you must use your mouth as an offensive weapon to say what God says. Just like believing, this is all an act of your will. Aligning your mouth with God's Word does not mean that you are in denial of the facts of your situation; it simply means that you choose to agree with God's perspective.

Think of it this way: Your life may be in turmoil in every area. You can choose to reinforce the facts or you can agree with how God sees your situation and declare out of your mouth, *"You, Lord, give true peace to those who depend on you, because they trust you"* (Isaiah 26:3 NCV). Agreeing with God's Word gives God permission to enter your situation and change it for His purposes.

This process will not be without its challenges because the devil will attack every righteous resolve. The moment you begin the faith process, the devil will try to weaken your resolve through doubt. You must fight the good fight of faith: *"Fight the good fight of faith, lay hold on eternal life, to which you were also called and have confessed the good confession in the presence of many witnesses"* (1 Timothy 6:12 NKJ).

You are not necessarily fighting with the devil, but you are fighting his encroachments on your thought life! Thoughts will be planted in your mind that will suggest that you give up or turn back.

Resourcefulness Principles

The Bible is clear that you are in a fight! You must hold fast. You cannot give up (2 Corinthians 10:3-5).

Other people can also serve as hindrances. People's misunderstanding of the faith process and their objections to your walking by faith can serve as an intimidation factor in your development. If others intimidate you, your resolve will weaken. Over time, you will confess God's Word less and less in response to their disapproval. Discouragement can mount because of the amount of time that it takes for the faith process to manifest the completed results. (Tomorrow you will learn about the importance of patience.) Don't waver in your resolve! Counteract every feeling of frustration with a bold action response. You will recall that the faith walk is a disciplined walk. You must force yourself to stay in faith when everything within you or everyone around you says, "Stop!" According to Romans 4:18, Abraham hoped against hope and he is our example of tenacious faith.

Even if your situation gets worse, you cannot weaken your resolve. You should keep confessing what God says until you can see it with your natural eyes. Your words should always be backed up with bold action.

In the faith process, this is called corresponding action. Your actions should correspond with the faith you confess. During the ministry of Jesus, He would speak a bold declaration of faith and expect the person to do something in agreement with what He said. As it relates to faith, faith is not biblical faith if there is no corresponding action! You will find in life that there are different types of people as it relates to the faith walk.

There are *anti-faith* people who oppose the notion that you can speak God's Word and see change. They are against people who

Day 12 - Words and Works

teach faith and those who walk by faith. Others have *argumentative faith*. These people argue over how faith should be executed. They want to debate the roles that confession, prayer, and action have in working together. The problem with this group is that they never act on faith; they just debate it.

Still another group of people have *academic faith*. They have studied the great faith teachers and the message of faith. They can trace the biblical foundations of the faith movement. But their study never translates into faith action. They will say, "Oh, I know that confession stuff but I don't do it." A closely related group is the *articulate faith* people. They talk about faith. They know the components. They have testimonies about others who used the faith process, but they never walk by faith themselves. Then, you have people who possess *admiration faith*. They will cling to you as you take this journey. They will be cheerleaders for you as you confess the Word of God and stand in faith. As you Maximize Your Life, they will rejoice with you at every victory. Yet they won't do it for themselves.

A Maximizer possesses *action faith*! That's when you are willing to act on Scripture and stand until you see results. Regardless of the opposition of the devil, other people, or circumstances, you continue to walk by faith and not by sight!

Remember Joshua? He received a Word from God that would bring him and the children of Israel great victory: *"Now the gates of Jericho were tightly shut because the people were afraid of the Israelites. No one was allowed to go out or in. But the Lord said to Joshua, 'I have given you Jericho, its king, and all its strong warriors. You and your fighting men should march around the town once a day for six days. Seven priests will walk ahead of the Ark, each carrying a ram's*

Resourcefulness Principles

horn. On the seventh day you are to march around the town seven times, with the priests blowing the horns. When you hear the priests give one long blast on the rams' horns, have all the people shout as loud as they can. Then the walls of the town will collapse, and the people can charge straight into the town.' So Joshua called together the priests and said, 'Take up the Ark of the Lord's Covenant, and assign seven priests to walk in front of it, each carrying a ram's horn'" (Joshua 6:1-6 NLT).

Even though the instructions from God went against traditional military strategy, Joshua and the people *did* what God had said. And you know how it all ended: The walls—the impenetrable walls—came down. In order to operate in faith, you must have the discipline to obey the Word of God and the voice of God.

The woman with the issue of blood is another biblical example: *"In the crowd was a woman who had been bleeding for twelve years. She had gone to many doctors, and they had not done anything except cause her a lot of pain. She had paid them all the money she had. But instead of getting better, she only got worse. The woman had heard about Jesus, so she came up behind him in the crowd and barely touched his clothes. She had said to herself, 'If I can just touch his clothes, I will get well.' As soon as she touched them, her bleeding stopped, and she knew she was well"* (Mark 5:25-29 CEV). She not only said what she believed, but she acted on it—even to the extent of breaking religious restrictions. She followed her confession with bold, determined action. And the condition that plagued her for 12 years left!

There are those who think their words and actions do not have to agree. Here is what the Bible pronounces on that thought process: *"You foolish person! Must you be shown that faith that does*

Day 12 - Words and Works

nothing is worth nothing" (James 2:20 NCV)? Your words and your works must line up! When they do, you will see the manifestation of your faith.

Maximized Prayer:
Father, faith without works is invalid! I commit today to add action to my confession so that I can walk the Maximized Life Journey successfully. Help me keep a guard over my mouth! In Jesus' name, Amen.

Maximizing Moments:
What kind of words have you been speaking? (Evaluate what you say in prayer and what you say in casual conversation.) If there is not consistent confession, then your faith will not work.

Do your actions line up with your faith? If not, what will you do to change them?

Maximizing Mantra:
The Word of God works through my confession and conduct.

Notes

Day 13 – Be Obedient & Patient

*"If you willingly obey me,
the best crops in the land will be yours."*
Isaiah 1:19 (CEV)

There are rewards to obedience. In fact, God's best only comes through obedience. Obedience is a learned behavior. When you do what God tells you to do, you will always receive from God's abundant storehouse. The choice to obey God is the choice to spend your days enjoying the best that God has to offer: *"If they listen and obey God, they will be blessed with prosperity throughout their lives. All their years will be pleasant"* (Job 36:11 NLT). As you continue on this journey, you must have a willingness and readiness to obey God's instructions.

There is no substitute for obedience—though many wish there were! God's divine power is always the end result of obedience. Your success in life depends on your obedience. Obedience is defined as a calculated choice to comply and carry out the will of God. There are three types of obedience: constrained, partial, and willful. Constrained obedience is forced obedience that is imposed because of circumstances, age, or other outside confinements. The will is not involved, but obedience is imposed on the Believer by external forces (not God). Partial obedience is where many people live. You should know that, ultimately, partial obedience is disobedience. Following most of what God says will not lead you to the Maximized Life you seek. The only way that you will succeed is through willful obedience. This is the pathway to promotion.

So what will it take for you to walk in willful obedience? First, you will need to accept God as the most significant Being in your life. The one who is the most important will have the most influence and the right to give you instructions. If someone else occupies this role, you will find it very difficult to obey God. If acceptance from God alone is your priority, then you will be able to operate in consistent obedience. If, on the other hand, you need acceptance from anyone else, you will be prone to compromise! This will nullify your ability to make bold moves for God. God will ask you to take moves that others will not understand and their inability to understand does not negate what God told you.

Next, you will need to take actions, bold steps of obedience, without full or complete understanding. You will recall yesterday we looked at Joshua and his walk around the walls of Jericho. God's instructions to him were unusual and held no military merit—so one would think. Yet, even though Joshua did not fully understand the instruction, he obeyed it. And God kept His Word. God will never tell you to do anything that violates His will or your integrity and witness.

Also, you should be very aware that you will come under attack for your obedience to God. You must determine to confront every mental argument and contrary thought that causes you to question God's will. Contrary thoughts will attack you. Expect it and prepare in advance to aggressively respond with faith-filled words!

Last, you should appropriate the power of God to help you to obey. This is called grace! When the pressure mounts, you will need to declare this grace over your life to keep you in a state of obedience. You cannot turn back once you have stepped out in faith. You will lose your momentum. Remember, the devil wants you to get out of obedience because he knows you will never receive God's best in a state of disobedience. Make the commitment to obey God—no matter how long it takes for your faith to manifest results.

Day 13 – Be Obedient & Patient

If you are willing to stand in faith forever, you will not have to! Some people try to give God a deadline, thinking that they can manipulate Him into acting on their behalf. This will not work! (After all, God has been around longer than you! He has heard every trick before and is impervious to them.) This is where patience comes in.

Patience is a partner to faith. Most people do not understand patience. Most people think patience is standing around waiting for something to happen. However, that is not biblical patience. Patience is shown when *"you do not become sluggish, but imitate those who through faith and patience inherit the promises"* (Hebrews 6:12 NKJ). Patience cannot compromise zeal, anticipation, expectation, or your confession. Patience is not resigning from the fight but a determination to keep on fighting while there are no visible victories. Patience is not a cop-out covered in religious language. So many Christians become tired in the fight and, having lost their resolve, declare that God released them from the faith commitment. The truth is those persons quit prematurely.

You are not a quitter! Patience is an active force of perseverance, endurance, fortitude, and persistence. None of these words sounds like giving up. Patience is a force of action that does not distract you from your corresponding action but undergirds it. With the force of patience, you possess a greater tenacity to succeed:

"By your steadfastness and patient endurance you shall win the true life of your souls." (Luke 21:19 AMP)

"To those who by patience in well-doing seek for glory and honor and immortality, he will give eternal life." (Romans 2:7 ESV)

Resourcefulness Principles

"And not only that, but we also glory in tribulations, knowing that tribulation produces perseverance; and perseverance, character; and character, hope." (Romans 5:3-4 NKJ)

You are not waiting to see what happens. As a Maximizer, you are making things happen! You may have to make some changes, but you should not sit back and do nothing. Patience is the spiritual resolve that gives birth to the strength and the tenacity necessary to fight through opportunities to quit! You can give up but you choose not to! Always remember, *"For you have need of endurance, so that after you have done the will of God, you may receive the promise"* (Hebrews 10:36 NKJ). You will receive everything that God has promised if you obey and walk in patient endurance.

Maximized Prayer:
Father, You are first place in my life! I set my will to obey You in all things. While I am obeying You, I will be patient because I know You will keep Your Word. In Jesus' name, Amen.

Maximizing Moments:
Take some time and discover what usually prompts you to quit. Once you identify these, write them down. Then create a contingency plan, which will allow you to stay the course when those quitting cues arise.

Maximizing Mantra:
Through faith and patience, I inherit the promises of God!

Day 14 – Don't Stop Believing

"But we live by faith, not by what we see."
2 Corinthians 5:7 (CEV)

Faith is not magic! It is a systematic spiritual process that creates God's will in your life. Faith can change anything, but faith must be exercised for it to work. Today you are going to learn eight (8) steps to exercising your faith on a continual basis. (You already learned the components to the faith process. These will be the practical steps that you take to keep your faith growing.) As you put these into practice daily, you will see transformation take place in your life. Your faith holds the key to what you will receive from God.

Faith is not difficult to understand once you have been taught what it is and how to operate in it. At the outset, understand that faith is a principle or a law! The reason why I say that faith is a spiritual principle is because the Bible declares it to be a law: *"Where is boasting then? It is excluded. By what law? of works? Nay: but by the law of faith"* (Romans 3:27 KJV). As a law, it works all the time and it works devoid of emotions, demographics (race, gender, nationality, and location), and opposition. Faith is as consistent as gravity and can be relied upon all the time.

Since faith cannot be activated without the Word of God, your faith journey starts when you *find the promise in the Bible*. If your request cannot be found in the Bible, faith cannot produce it. However, if you can find the promise, then God is obligated to manifest it according to your faith. As you read the Bible, you will find that God's promises cover every area of your life. God is more than willing to keep His Word: *"For with God nothing is ever impossible and no word from God shall be without power or impossible of fulfillment"* (Luke 1:37 AMP). God backs up His Word with His

Resourcefulness Principles

power. This is what establishes your expectation. If God made a promise, then He wrote it for a reason. He wants you to have it. Often people have stated that God is mysterious. However, if God wanted to be mysterious, He wouldn't have written the Bible. While we may never know *how* God does what He does, we are very clear about what God will do because the Bible informs us.

Once you have located the promise in the Bible, you then should *make the quality decision to believe what God's Word says.* This may sound simplistic, but so many Christians read the Bible and see what God has promised but automatically exclude themselves. For instance, the Bible says, *"For God has not given us a spirit of fear and timidity, but of power, love, and self-discipline"* (2 Timothy 2:7 NLT). At the point at which you read this, you can choose to say, "I know that is what the Bible says, but I do not feel like I have power because I am overcome with fear"; or you can choose to say, "In spite of the feelings of fear that are gripping me, I believe what the Word of God says and I have a spirit of power, love and a sound mind!" Don't exclude yourself; include yourself! The Bible was written for you! Receive its promises and you will see a great change in your life. Choose to believe!

Having made the choice to believe, you should continually *sow God's Word into your heart.* The choice to believe must be fortified by repeated hearing of the Word of God. Faith is a matter of the heart! If fear or doubt resides in your heart, it will work against you! Repeatedly sowing Scripture into your heart will drive out any second-guessing that may exist. Faith comes to the Believer in one way: *"So then faith cometh by hearing, and hearing by the word of God"* (Romans 10:17 KJV). You should set a daily routine of hearing, on

Day 14 - Don't Stop Believing

average, at least one (1) hour of Bible teaching daily. This will establish you in the Truth of God's Word.

Then, you are encouraged to *keep your thought life in agreement with God's Word*. The greatest battlefield for the Believer is the arena of the mind. Your mind, until it has been renewed, will fight against faith! Bringing your wayward thoughts back into alignment with God's Word is the only way you will win the battle of the mind. As a general rule, you should never articulate a negative thought that contradicts the promises in the Word of God. You will *"capture every thought and make it give up and obey Christ"* (2 Corinthians 10:5 NCV). You will learn a method to do this later in the Maximized Life Journey. For today you should reject immediately any thought that does not reinforce God's Word.

Very closely tied with your thought life is your conversation or speech life. Faith is released by the words of your mouth. So, as you win the battle of the mind, you will find the importance of *releasing faith by speaking God's Word*. Your words have power to change your life! In fact, your life is the sum total of the words that you have spoken. When you are uncertain what to say, speak the Word of God. Rehearse the promises of God verbally. Your words are very powerful. As your mouth aligns with God's Word, so will your life. This is called confession. (This is another topic that we will look at in more detail starting on Day 43.)

What you really believe, you will act on. When you are standing in faith for God to do something, you will need to *act like the Word is so*. This corresponding action will bring your faith to life. Faith is an action word. When you act on the Word, you marshal heaven's forces to assist you. If you truly believe that God's promises are true, then you will act on them, right? This is not a one-time event. You

Resourcefulness Principles

should keep on acting on the Word of God until you see in reality what you believe God for.

While you are acting on the Word of God by faith, you will *offer the sacrifice of praise to God continually.* Because you do not have any visual evidence, you will be praising God by faith (sacrifice). You will praise God for keeping His Word and what you know He has already done based on His promises! Praise is a dynamic, vocal expression of love, adoration, and appreciation to God. God loves to hear the praise of His children. As you praise God, you invite Him into your situation to encourage you and strengthen you. This strength will be important because the last step in exercising your faith is *waiting patiently for manifestation.*

You have learned some very critical information today that will give more meaning to your Journey. Tomorrow we will talk about the five (5) expectations of faith.

Maximized Prayer:
Father, I must do my part in the faith process in order to see results. I trust the process and know that the law of faith must work on my behalf. In Jesus' name, Amen.

Maximizing Moments:
Have you been exercising your faith?

What have you intentionally done to stay in an attitude of faith?

Maximizing Mantra:
I work my faith every day!

Day 15 – Faith Works

*"The earth produces the crops on its own.
First a leaf blade pushes through,
then the heads of wheat are formed,
and finally the grain ripens."*
Mark 4:28 (NLT)

So what can you expect while you are walking by faith and exercising patience? As you will recall, faith is a process and its results are progressive. You cannot be discouraged because the full manifestation of your faith does not show up all at once. In fact, the Bible never promises that it will show up at once. As the Scripture for today shows us, the results are progressive, just like crops that grow in the fields.

Faith is an incremental spiritual and natural process. The good thing about this process is that you do not need to know how it works. Many Believers give undue attention to "how" God will do what He promised. This is a waste of time! You do not need to know how! Think of how many things around you that work perfectly well but you have no idea how they work.

When you put the key into the ignition of the car, you do not need to know how the engine works to get the car to drive. When you board a plane, you may not be able to understand the laws of lift, thrust, gravity, and drag; but you have a confidence that the plane under the direction of the pilot will land safely. The phone or computer that you use regularly is another good example. There are so many components and processes running that only an engineer can understand the full inner workings of the electronic device. However, not knowing how it works does not stop you from using it for full benefit. The list can go on and on.

The same is true of faith! You do not need to know how faith brings about change. You just need to know that it works in every situation. You cannot minimize God down to what you can figure out. That is not faith; it is reasoning on tiptoes!

God calls us to walk in a genuine faith that trusts Him completely! When we approach faith this way, it leaves the door open for God to be God! This is why faith is not magic! You will see steady progress. The manifestation will not happen overnight (though we always leave the option open for God to perform a miracle.) When the miraculous takes place, it is a supernatural intervention of God where He suspends natural law to bring His will to pass. The challenge is that you cannot predict a miracle. While you cannot predict a miracle, you can predict the outcome of your faith. So what can you expect?

There are five (5) expectations that you should have as a result of obeying God. The first is a plan of action! God will give you action steps (these could come from the Bible, from a deliberate thought process, or from another person's example). Do not undervalue the necessity of a plan because God knows how to bless plans and bring them to successful conclusions. The second result of faith is the divine favor of God. Favor is someone using his or her power, influence, and ability to help you. You learned earlier that partnership is a part of God's plan. God will bring you to the top of the pile. God will put you on someone's mind. God can move on the heart of total strangers to act on your behalf. Your faith victory is no less valuable because someone helps you.

God can give you divine wisdom. Wisdom is the right application of knowledge. You may have all the pieces, but God will show you how to put them together to gain the desired result. God's

Day 15 - Faith Works

wisdom may lead you to a person who has your answers. God will not leave you helpless as you stand in faith. You can also expect a miracle. But remember what we mentioned before about the unpredictability of miracles, they work as the Spirit wills and not as the person wills. (They are hard to plan for!) Last, you can expect that God will give you strength to endure! As you go through, God will encourage you on the journey! As your flesh becomes weak and those give-up opportunities increase, you will sense an inexplicable peace and strength rise within you to give you the fortitude to stay the course.

Since you know faith will work for you, remain in expectation for one of its five (5) manifestations. You now just need to REST: *"So there is a special rest still waiting for the people of God. For all who have entered into God's rest have rested from their labors, just as God did after creating the world. So let us do our best to enter that rest. But if we disobey God, as the people of Israel did, we will fall"* (Hebrews 4:9-11 NLT).

In order to enter this rest, it will take some work. First, you will have to *renew your mind towards your situation.* You will learn some strategies later in this journey. For now you should know that you must saturate your mind with the Word of God! What is the main input into your life? Whatever that is will govern your thought process. If television news, newspapers, and Internet sites are the major input into your life, they will set your thought processes. You will not have the mental fortitude to stay on course with your faith. Have a daily regimen of hearing the Word of God taught. As you listen, your mind will be changed to more readily accept God's thoughts and not human thoughts.

Resourcefulness Principles

Next, you should *endure the temporary condition, knowing that it lasts only for a little while.* Whatever you can see with your natural eye is subject to change! Do not be deceived into thinking that your situation will last forever because it won't! You have to outlast the situation, and you are well able to because *"the temptations in your life are no different from what others experience. And God is faithful. He will not allow the temptation to be more than you can stand. When you are tempted, he will show you a way out so that you can endure"* (1 Corinthians 10:13 NLT). When you are ready to give up, so is the devil. Just outlast him! You are well able to do it!

While you are enduring, you should stand on God's Word until the promise manifests. You have learned about patience. When you have done all you know to do, *"stand strong, with the belt of truth tied around your waist and the protection of right living on your chest"* (Ephesians 6:14 NCV). Your standing is possible because you are a prayer warrior. (You will read about this for the next couple of days.) Then, you will *trust God for the end results because He is Your Deliverer!*

It's now time to

    R - Renew your mind.

    E - Endure the condition.

    S - Stand on God's Word.

    T - Trust God for results.

Day 15 - Faith Works

Maximized Prayer:
>Father, You are always working on my behalf! I REST in You because you are truly my Deliverer! You will always come through for me. In Jesus' name, Amen.

Maximizing Moments:
>Have you missed when God was trying to give you results of your faith? (You were expecting one thing and God sent something else?)
>
>What are some things that you can intentionally do to put your mind at peace while you are in expectation?

Maximizing Mantra:
>My faith is working!

Notes

Day 16 – Stop the Prayer Blockers

"And it came to pass, that, as he was praying in a certain place, when he ceased, one of his disciples said unto him, Lord, teach us to pray, as John also taught his disciples."
Luke 11:1 (KJV)

Prayer to many people is a mystery. They often wonder, "How can I get God to answer my prayers? Why does God seem to answer the prayers of others and not mine?" Questions abound because, as simple as God made prayer, many have complicated it. However, once you as a Maximizer understand the importance of prayer and the biblical way to pray, you will gain great joy in praying!

While prayer is important to the Believer, your body and mind will not readily cooperate. When you set aside time to pray, you will be interrupted by random thoughts and reminders of things to do. You may have just awakened, but an inexplicable fatigue will overcome you. Outside forces will conspire to steal your prayer time no matter when you schedule it or make time for it. This should not surprise you! Have a strategy to overcome these and other distractions.

So what is prayer? Prayer is the channel of communication between the Believer and God whereby God's power is released into the earth realm through the combination of the Believer's faith and the Word of God. Prayer is all about results! God gave us prayer so that we have a means by which to communicate with Him and God has a method by which to accomplish His will in the earth (including your life). Maximizers pray effectively. After all, that's the only way to pray.

I have become convinced that prayerlessness in the life of the Believer is because of a lack of results! When we do not see the value

Regimen of Prayer

in something, it is very difficult to remain faithful to do it. As we see fewer results, we pray less and less until we stop praying!

Prayerlessness is sin! Jesus' taught His disciples that *"they should always pray and never give up"* (Luke 18:1 NLT). So, if prayer is so powerful and God wants you to pray, why aren't your prayers answered?

Here are some common barriers to answered prayer:

Unbelief undermines the effectiveness of prayer. Jesus gave specific instructions about prayer: *"Whatever things you ask when you pray, believe that you receive them, and you will have them"* (Mark 11:24 KJV). The only prayers that are answered are those prayers that are backed up with belief. If you do not believe that your prayers will be answered, then they won't. Unbelief also extends to the content of the prayer. God is only obligated to answer prayers that are according to His will. So, if your prayers are not based in God's Word, He does not hear them.

Selfishness undermines the attitude of prayer. As you learned about purpose, it is never just about you! If your prayers are always focused on your life, your needs, and your advancement, then you have violated the heart of God concerning prayer. As we learned earlier, prayer licenses God to work in the earth. God wants to work for more than just you! A Maximizer has a heart to see others blessed and moving forward on their journeys. Selfishness violates the law of love and cancels your prayers.

Retaliation undermines the intent of prayer. We have all gone through situations where people have wronged us and their guilt is indisputable. Yet we can never pray for God to get even with anyone. Prayers of retaliation are wasted words that God does not hear. God loves the person who hurt you as much as He loves you. God is being patient with them just as He has been patient with you: *"He does not want anyone to be lost, but he wants all people to change their hearts and lives"* (2 Peter 3:9 NCV).

Years ago, I had to learn this lesson when faced with the lies and misrepresentations of others. God told me that my vindication does not come from the harm that comes to others. My vindication comes from God's continued blessing on my life. And God said that He would let my enemies live long enough to see me blessed. David demonstrated that he understood this when He declared, *"You treat me to a feast, while my enemies watch. You honor me as your guest and you fill my cup until it overflows"* (Psalm 23:5 CEV).

Unforgiveness and unconfessed sins undermine the results of prayer. Harboring resentment and hiding transgressions hinder our prayers: *"And whenever you stand praying, if you have anything against anyone, forgive him and let it drop (leave it, let it go), in order that your Father Who is in heaven may also forgive you your [own] failings and shortcomings and let them drop"* (Mark 11:25 AMP). Unforgiveness blocks the flow of forgiveness into our lives. Forgiveness is a decision not to penalize someone for what has been done. It is never your responsibility to punish people for the wrongs they commit. The Bible commands that you forgive others.

Unconfessed sins are another area that blocks the results of prayer. To sin is to transgress against God and His Word. Unconfessed or unrepented sin disconnects you from all that God has prepared for you. God has zero tolerance for sin in your life: *"Your iniquities have turned these blessings away, and your sins have kept good [harvests] from you"* (Jeremiah 5:25 AMP). Sin is counteracted by repentance and forgiveness. We ask God for

Regimen of Prayer

forgiveness, and we turn away (repent) from the sinful activity. The promise you have is, *"But if we confess our sins, he will forgive our sins, because we can trust God to do what is right. He will cleanse us from all the wrongs we have done"* (1 John 1:9 NCV).

A hypocritical relationship with God undermines the credibility of our prayers. Because God is authentic and true, He cannot be fooled or have the wool pulled over His eyes. He sees everything and knows everything. When we feign a relationship with God that does not exist, it may make us feel good; but it has no spiritual value at all: *"When you pray, don't be like those show-offs who love to stand up and pray in the meeting places and on the street corners. They do this just to look good. I can assure you that they already have their reward"* (Matthew 6:5 CEV).

When you are more concerned about the applause of people than pleasing God, your prayers will not have credibility with God. People may like them, but God ignores them.

Last, *physical fatigue undermines the fulfillment of prayer.* You can certainly attest to the fact that sleepiness is an enemy to a joyous and fulfilling prayer life. Can you imagine getting a private audience with the president of the United States and, as soon as you sit in the Oval Office, you fall asleep? Well, the God of the Universe has given us an open door to come into His Presence and talk with Him whenever we are ready. How can we allow fatigue to ruin that time? When you see prayer as tedious and unfulfilling, you will succumb to those tired sensations every time. But, when you see prayer as a vital communications link to God that will change situations in life, you will fight all hints of boredom and fatigue so that you can get the most out of prayer.

Day 16 - Stop the Prayer Blockers

We must be intentional about removing all the hindrances to prayer because prayer works! And, to be honest, we need the results of prayer working in our lives. In order to Maximize Your Life, prayer—effective prayer—will strengthen you for the journey and produce lasting results. Tomorrow you will learn some of the barriers that have kept your prayers from being effective.

Maximized Prayer:
Father, I repent of every hindrance that has produced barriers to my answered prayers. I ask that You forgive me for all unforgiveness and every sin in my life. I embrace a vibrant, fulfilling prayer life from this day forward. In Jesus' name, Amen.

Maximizing Moments:
What hindrances have you identified to your prayers?

Are there people you have not forgiven? If so, take time now to release them and resubmit your life to God.

Maximizing Mantra:
God answers all my prayers because I pray according to His Word!

Regimen of Prayer

NOTES

Day 17 – Prayer Works

"We are certain that God will hear our prayers when we ask for what pleases him. And if we know that God listens when we pray, we are sure that our prayers have already been answered."
1 John 5:14-15 (CEV)

Now that we have addressed the hindrances to an effective prayer life, it is important to fully understand the components of a healthy, results-oriented prayer life. You should have confidence in your prayer life and the benefits afforded you from prayer.

Our reading for today encourages us to understand the conditions under which God hears and answers prayers. Many people have been taught that God answers prayer in three ways: yes, no, and wait. There is no biblical example for this type of theology. In fact, the Bible teaches us that God hears and answers affirmatively every prayer that is prayed according to His will. What is God's will? It's very simple: His Word! What God has promised and expressed in the Bible is the foundation for what we believe (you learned about this a couple of days ago). Your faith begins where the will of God is known!

Normally, when people talk about prayer, they do not use words like "certainly" and "surely"; more often than not, they use "hopefully," "probably," and "maybe." These words are not in God's lexicon. As vital as prayer is to your life, God wants to make certain that you have a confidence in its merits and its effectiveness on your life. If we can line our view of prayer up with God's view of prayer, then we can see great results from our prayer time.

Since you are supposed to have a dynamic prayer life, what should that prayer life look like? Here are some very simple tips that will cause you to have a remarkable prayer life.

Regimen of Prayer

Jesus taught His disciples how prayer should be modeled: *"After this manner therefore pray ye: Our Father which art in heaven, Hallowed be thy name. Thy kingdom come, Thy will be done in earth, as it is in heaven. Give us this day our daily bread. And forgive us our debts, as we forgive our debtors. And lead us not into temptation, but deliver us from evil: For thine is the kingdom, and the power, and the glory, for ever. Amen"* (Matthew 6:9-13 KJV).

Some have mistakenly thought that Jesus taught His disciples to pray this exact prayer. However, Jesus instructed them to pray *"after this manner"* or, as the Amplified Bible translates it, *"Pray, therefore, like this."* This is a model for prayer that all Believers should use.

This prayer begins with focusing on God as your Father and His magnificence. In this beginning part of your prayer time, you should intentionally praise your Heavenly Father for Who He is in your life. There is no asking during this time. It is all about acknowledging Who God is to you! This makes your prayer very personal and meaningful. As you worship God for Who He is to you and praise God for what He has done for you, you are actually reminding yourself that God can be trusted with whatever you are about to ask Him. You may find it helpful to call God by His other biblical names: Provider, Healer, Shepherd, Savior, Deliverer, etc. Focus your mind on the One to Whom you are praying. This first phase of prayer is the adoration phase.

You should be reminded that you should never pray to Jesus but to the Father in Jesus' name: *"This is what I want you to do: Ask the Father for whatever is in keeping with the things I've revealed to you. Ask in my name, according to my will, and he'll most certainly give it to you. Your joy will be a river overflowing its banks"* (John 16:23-24 MSG)!

Day 17 - Prayer Works

The second phase of prayer is the declaration phase. During your prayer time, you should declare God's will over your life, your family's life, the larger Body of Christ, your local church, and the civil government. God has made so many promises for your life and He stands behind all of them. By knowing God's biblical promises, you can keep yourself focused on exactly what God has promised to you in all situations. There is nothing that you will face for which God has not already provided a solution or promise. (On Days 43 through 45, you will learn how to proclaim God's Word for your life.)

Phase 3 is about our provisions: those things made available by God to meet any and every need that arises. Whether spiritual, physical, natural, social, or emotional, God has made provisions available to you! This is not the time to rehearse what is not working in your life. It is time to focus on what God's will is concerning those areas of your life! You may ask, "How can I be so bold in my prayer life?": *"So then, since we have a great High Priest who has entered heaven, Jesus the Son of God, let us hold firmly to what we believe. This High Priest of ours understands our weaknesses, for he faced all of the same testings we do, yet he did not sin. So let us come boldly to the throne of our gracious God. There we will receive his mercy, and we will find grace to help us when we need it most"* (Hebrews 4:14-16 NLT). Because of what Jesus has done for you, you can be bold in your prayers! It's okay! God can handle your boldness because He stands behind His Word!

Phase 4 of prayer is a time of personal reflection and evaluation. This is a time for honest introspection about actions, words, and thoughts. You should confess any sins, debts, and offenses that are in

Regimen of Prayer

your life. Once you have confessed your sins, receive the forgiveness so freely given by God.

We signal to God our willingness to learn without having to go through trials and tests. Because we have an adversary who seeks to destroy us, we should also use this phase as a time of spiritual warfare. We use the authority given to us by Jesus to relent every encroachment of evil and satanic oppression in our lives and the lives of others. You have been given this authority legitimately from Jesus: *"And I will give you the keys of the Kingdom of Heaven. Whatever you forbid on earth will be forbidden in heaven, and whatever you permit on earth will be permitted in heaven"* (Matthew 16:19 MSG).

Believers seldom use the authority entrusted to them. Not you, though, because you are a Maximizer! This is an exciting and engaging period during your prayer time because you are on the offensive concerning your prayer concerns.

The last phase is a closing time of praise and worship. Here, you thank God for hearing and acting on your behalf as He promised. With this time finished, you end your prayer time with a great sense of peace, knowing that God is on your side and Heaven is backing you in your Maximized Life Journey.

Maximized Prayer:

Father, communicating with You was always meant to be exciting, fulfilling, and effective. I repent for taking this time for granted and I commit to live a life of prayer. In Jesus' name, Amen.

Maximizing Moments:

What are the dominant traits of God for which you are thankful?

What role does complaining or worrying play in your prayer life?

What are the key areas in which you need the intervention of God?

What promises are you relying upon as you take this journey?

Maximizing Mantra:

I come boldly to God's throne and find grace to help me in the time of trouble!

NOTES

Day 18 – It's All Good

"Until now you have not asked for anything in my name. Ask and you will receive, so that your joy will be the fullest possible joy."
John 16:24 (NCV)

As you focus on your prayer life, you can begin to see the crucial role that prayer plays in making your journey effective. Today we are going to look at the results that occur because of our active prayer life.

There are only good results that come from prayer. Your commitment to a lifestyle of personal devotion and prayer is critical to experiencing the Maximized Life that Jesus died to give you. Today I want you to focus on the benefits of a dedicated prayer life.

Prayer causes breakthrough revelation. Prayer is a special time when God reveals *things that are critical to your destiny and quality of life: "Ask me and I will tell you remarkable secrets you do not know about things to come"* (Jeremiah 33:3 NLT). We all celebrate that God is all-knowing (omniscient). However, God wants to reveal what He knows to us! (This is one of the great benefits of Christianity. God wants His children to know about their future and what He has planned for them.) God is not as mysterious as we have made Him out to be! He is a Revealer of mysteries.

When your heart is right towards God and your desire is to please Him, God is obligated to bring you into the knowledge of the things you need to know and the company of the people you need to know that are crucial to your destiny in life! Prayer is a medium through which God speaks to us.

God speaks to us by way of the Holy Spirit, in two primary ways. First, He speaks through His Word. God will take you to a Scripture or remind you of a biblical example that is relevant to your

Regimen of Prayer

situation. God will never speak to you in a manner contrary to His Word. This is the primary way that God will reveal information to His children.

God also speaks through your thought life. God will grant you creative ideas and give you wisdom and insight into things that you are facing. God may give you a new perspective on an old situation (1 Corinthians 2:9-10). Please be reminded that if your thoughts do not align with God's written word, those thoughts should be rejected immediately.

Prayer causes barriers to be removed. On the Maximized Life Journey, barriers will appear. Prayer is the primary weapon to remove those barriers from your path. Roadblocks should not be permanent impediments but temporary hurdles to be overcome! No matter how restrictive or daunting the barriers may appear, your diligent prayer life can overcome them.

One biblical account that amazes me and shows how earnest heartfelt prayer can bring supernatural deliverance and the release from barriers is the story of Paul and Silas: *"The judges went along with the mob, had Paul and Silas's clothes ripped off and ordered a public beating. After beating them black-and-blue, they threw them into jail, telling the jailkeeper to put them under heavy guard so there would be no chance of escape. He did just that—threw them into the maximum security cell in the jail and clamped leg irons on them. Along about midnight, Paul and Silas were at prayer and singing a robust hymn to God. The other prisoners couldn't believe their ears. Then, without warning, a huge earthquake! The jailhouse tottered, every door flew open, all the prisoners were loose. Startled from sleep, the jailer saw all the doors swinging loose on their hinges. Assuming that all the prisoners had escaped, he pulled out his sword and was about to do*

Day 18 - It's All Good

himself in, figuring he was as good as dead anyway, when Paul stopped him: 'Don't do that! We're all still here! Nobody's run away!' The jailer got a torch and ran inside. Badly shaken, he collapsed in front of Paul and Silas. He led them out of the jail and asked, 'Sirs, what do I have to do to be saved, to really live?' They said, 'Put your entire trust in the Master Jesus. Then you'll live as you were meant to live—and everyone in your house included'" (Acts 16:23-31 MSG)!

Here is a clear example of how prayer can remove seemingly insurmountable barriers (prison door and chains). There are many other examples in the Bible. The God to whom you pray can remove any barrier, open any door.

Prayer causes barrenness to be reversed. Do you find yourself in a barren or unproductive situation? Prayer reverses situations. Barrenness is a state of non-fruit bearing. It is the will of God for you to be productive and bring forth more fruit. Regardless of what you have already done, you can do more. Are you facing a period of barrenness? There is a remedy: prayer!

In the Old Testament, a mother's barrenness was overcome through prayer. In fact, she gave birth to one of the greatest prophets in the Bible. Hannah was unable to give birth. She cried out to God earnestly to reverse her unproductive state: *"Once after a sacrificial meal at Shiloh, Hannah got up and went to pray. Eli the priest was sitting at his customary place beside the entrance of the Tabernacle. Hannah was in deep anguish, crying bitterly as she prayed to the Lord. And she made this vow: 'O Lord of Heaven's Armies, if you will look upon my sorrow and answer my prayer and give me a son, then I will give him back to you. He will be yours for his entire lifetime, and as a sign that he has been dedicated to the Lord, his hair will never be cut'"* (1 Samuel 1:9-11 NLT). Because of the fervency of her

Regimen of Prayer

prayers, Eli assumed that she was drunk. Hannah explained her plight and Eli sent her away with a blessing. Shortly thereafter, Hannah gave birth to Samuel. What a wonderful testament of God's power to reverse barrenness!

Why would you not want to tap into this barren-reversing power? Your prayer life makes this possible. The time that you spend praying will serve as the investment in maximizing your life. Allow the power of God, released through prayer, to counteract barrenness in any—and every—area of your life!

Prayer causes blessings to be released. The Bible teaches that God promises to make certain things happen in the earth in response to the prayers of His people. When you know that prayer will cause the specific promises of God to come to pass, you should possess an excitement about your prayer time. Let's review some of the scriptural passages that affirm God's promises for those who pray:

"Ask, and it shall be given you; seek, and ye shall find; knock, and it shall be opened unto you: For every one that asketh receiveth; and he that seeketh findeth; and to him that knocketh it shall be opened." (Matthew 7:7-8 KJV)

"If you remain in me and follow my teachings, you can ask anything you want, and it will be given to you. You should produce much fruit and show that you are my followers, which brings glory to my Father." (John 15:7-8 NCV)

"Then if my people who are called by my name will humble themselves and pray and seek my face and turn from their wicked ways, I will hear from heaven and will forgive their sins and restore their land." (2 Chronicles 7:14 CEV)

Day 18 - It's All Good

"And let us not grow weary while doing good, for in due season we shall reap if we do not lose heart." (Galatians 6:9 NKJ)

The most important element about building an effective prayer life is the commitment to be consistent in praying even when it looks like nothing is happening. I call this a commitment to tenacious prayer. I am sure that, if you will give yourself to a persevering commitment to pray, the experience of a Maximized Life will be seen in every area of your life.

Use the phases that you learned yesterday to guide your prayer time, and they will overcome the feelings of intimidation that attacks your prayer life. Don't forget: The benefits of prayer are all good!

Maximized Prayer:

Father, I understand the benefits of a prayer-filled life. I embrace this life as my own. I know that prayer was important to Jesus' life and prayer must be important to my life. I commit myself to a lifestyle of prayer in order to receive all the good blessings that come from prayer. In Jesus' name, Amen.

Maximizing Moments:

What are some of the benefits that you need from your prayer time?

Is there a Scripture on prayer that really speaks to your heart? (Memorize this and use it as a motivator when attacks come against your prayer life.)

Will you commit to a tenacious prayer regimen as a part of your Maximized Life Journey?

Maximizing Mantra:

My earnest prayer has great power and produces wonderful results.

DAY 19 – BE PROSPERITY MINDED

"Let them shout for joy and be glad, Who favor my righteous cause; And let them say continually, 'Let the LORD be magnified, Who has pleasure in the prosperity of His servant."
Psalm 35:27 (NKJ)

God's desire for you is increase—in every area, at all times! Maximizers possess an unshakable and irrevocable conviction that God's best for their lives is increase (prosperity): *"Beloved, I pray that you may prosper in all things and be in health, just as your soul prospers"* (3 John 2 KJV). To *prosper* means to "be successful." Isn't it good to know that God wants you to be successful: spiritually, emotionally, financially, and physically?

You will be successful to the degree that you condition your mind to accept this truth. So many people resist the notion of biblical prosperity. However, the alternative to prosperity is failure! If you are honest, that's what you have experienced at various points in your life. And, to be sure, your testimony of those times is that they did not feel good or normal. That is because from the beginning of creation, you were destined to be on top. God has nothing but great things in store for you: *"I know what I'm doing. I have it all planned out—plans to take care of you, not abandon you, plans to give you the future you hope for"* (Jeremiah 29:11 MSG).

God has a vested interest in your success and is eager to see you do well. So why are so many people afraid of this term *prosperity*? Many people have demonized the word prosperity to the extent that Believers have become timid about wanting to be successful in life! And this same group of people has tried to convince you that you should struggle in life and accept whatever life gives you. However, you know better because you are a Maximizer!

Revelation of Prosperity

Biblical prosperity is the fulfilled life (Maximized Life) where all needs—natural, spiritual and emotional—are met as a result of righteous, disciplined decision making that brings the will of God to pass in your life. Today you will gain a greater conviction about the blessings and prosperity that God desires for you:

"Oh, the joys of those who do not follow the advice of the wicked, or stand around with sinners, or join in with mockers. But they delight in the law of the Lord, meditating on it day and night. They are like trees planted along the riverbank, bearing fruit each season. Their leaves never wither, and they prosper in all they do." (Psalm 1:1-3 NLT)

"If they obey and serve him, the rest of their lives will be successful, and the rest of their years will be happy." (Job 36:11 NCV)

"The blessing of the Lord makes a person rich, and he adds no sorrow with it." (Proverbs 10:22 NLT)

"But remember the Lord your God! It is he who gives you the power to become rich, keeping the agreement he promised to your ancestors, as it is today." (Deuteronomy 8:18 NCV)

"Shout praises to the LORD! The LORD blesses everyone who worships him and gladly obeys his teachings. Their descendants will have great power in the land, because the LORD blesses all who do right. They will get rich and prosper and will always be remembered for their fairness." (Psalm 112:1-3 CEV)

"Teach those who are rich in this world not to be proud and not to trust in their money, which is so unreliable. Their trust should be in God, who richly gives us all we need for our enjoyment. Tell them to use their money to do good. They should be rich in good works and generous to those in need, always being ready to share with others." (1 Timothy 6:17-18 NLT)

Day 19 - Be Prosperity Minded

"For the LORD God is a sun and shield; The LORD will give grace and glory; No good thing will He withhold from those who walk uprightly." (Psalm 84:11 NKJ)

"Let them shout for joy and be glad, Who favor my righteous cause; And let them say continually, 'Let the LORD be magnified, Who has pleasure in the prosperity of His servant." (Psalm 35:27 NKJ)

"May the LORD give you increase more and more, You and your children." (Psalm 115:14 NKJ)

"Honour the LORD with thy substance, and with the firstfruits of all thine increase: So shall thy barns be filled with plenty, and thy presses shall burst out with new wine." (Proverbs 3:9-10 KJV)

"Seek the Kingdom of God above all else, and live righteously, and He will give you everything you need." (Matthew 6:33 NLT)

Based on the definition of prosperity and the Scriptures you've just read, you have a role to play in your prosperity. God wants you to succeed, but you have to cooperate with God's plan to prosper you. There are things that you can do to enhance your ability to prosper. If you want to live your life where your natural, spiritual, and emotional needs are met, it will require you to live your life in a way that pleases Him. The way that pleases God is righteous living.

Now it is true that Christians possess the gift of righteousness (Romans 10:3). However, God expects certain behavior from you as you live up to your righteous status: *"Awake to righteousness, and do not sin"* (1 Corinthians 15:34 NKJ). Righteousness is three-dimensional: You must possess a revelation of righteousness (the gift that God gives you at salvation), a disposition of righteousness (you must do right), and directional righteousness (you must be in the right place). If you are in a righteous state, you will have all your needs met.

The sum total of all the choices (decisions) that you have made in life will determine who you will be in life. You should choose to live righteously. Get the sin out of your life! Stop living below your status as a child of God! As soon as your behavior improves, you will be qualified for the blessings that God has promised. Today decide to be prosperity minded. Expect every need to be met! Expect to live in abundance! Expect to be successful! It is God's will for your life!

Maximized Prayer:
Father, I thank You in advance for the creative ideas and witty inventions that will change my financial situation. In Jesus' name, Amen.

Maximizing Moments:
What were you taught about prosperity? How were you taught to think about money?

What barriers to righteousness exist in your life?

Maximizing Mantra:
Wealth and riches are in my house.

Day 20 – Prosperity Explained

*"Lust for money brings trouble and nothing but trouble.
Going down that path, some lose their footing in the faith completely
and live to regret it bitterly ever after."*
1 Timothy 6:10 (MSG)

As you saw yesterday, the Bible is full of evidence to support the truth that God wants all His children living prosperous lives. However, there are those who will reject this truth and argue that prosperity is not God's will! You should know how to handle these objections because more often than not they will come from people who are in your circle of influence. People who are not Maximizers have corrupted thinking about prosperity, which makes them cynical, critical, and cheap!

Just to be clear, prosperity is available to the Believer but not essential to go to heaven! You can make the choice to live life struggling financially and you can still go to heaven when you die—and leave others to pay for your funeral. However, you will not have Maximized Your Life! Prosperity is for Believers who want all that God has promised.

The misconceptions about prosperity stem from misinformation promoted from both religious and worldly viewpoints. The cardinal objection to prosperity is the thinking that "money is evil!" Certainly you have heard someone espouse this erroneous statement. However, that is not what the Scripture says; it is the "lust for money" that is evil, not money! And there are ways that you can tell if you have a lust for money.

People lust for money if they measure their worth and the worth of others by it. There are those who must know what type of job you have, how much money you make, in what neighborhood you live, and what type of car you drive. These are subtle ways for them to determine your value and worth. This is such deficient thinking because self-worth is not equivalent to net worth! Every human's worth was determined at Calvary. The price that Jesus paid for humanity established its value! When self-worth is tied to net worth, as net worth changes, so will one's self-worth. For example, if someone has a lot of money, he or she will have a high self-worth. If that person's bank account balances are low, self-worth will be diminished. This is completely against God's view of His creation (Luke 12:15). These same lovers of money will treat people differently because their financial situation changes. They somehow think that their financial distress provides a rationale to mistreat people.

Others demonstrate a lust for money because they will do anything to get money. Whether it is lie, cheat, or steal, any behavior is acceptable if it ends in more money coming into their hands. (You would be surprised by the extent that people will go to get a dollar!) All of the "get rich quick" Internet schemes are based upon humanity's lust for money. Persons will throw away what little they have in an effort to get rich quickly! Some will violate the laws of God in order to advance financially.

Also, people demonstrate a lust for money when they make excuses not to support God's priorities. Giving is God's way! (You will learn more about this later in your journey.) When these people create excuses to withhold money from God's work, it's because they value money more than God. In a materialistic culture that is governed by conspicuous consumption, many, including Believers, have placed a higher premium on things and money than on serving God! This is why some in the family of God have rejected the message of prosperity. They are responding to the materialism that

Day 20 - Prosperity Explained

has crept into the Body of Christ. Maximizers understand the right use of money and how to keep it in perspective.

Money is a tool, a medium of exchange. Money mishandled will choke your commitment to righteousness. You should never sacrifice your spiritual service to pursue success or money.

Several things must be resolved if you are to handle money righteously and thus prequalify for prosperity:

- How do you handle the money you possess now?
- How far will you go to get money?
- How will you handle money when you have abundance?

When you answer these questions in light of what Scripture says, you qualify to receive financial increase (prosperity). God will never send prosperity to your life if you will mismanage it or allow it to become a god to you!

There are many ways to receive money; Scripture does not sanction all of them! However, there are biblical ways to receive money. The primary way to receive money is from work: legally working, not committing crimes like selling drugs or ponzi schemes, etc. Work is noble and the Bible unequivocally endorses work!

Another way to receive money is through gifts. These gifts should always be received with a God consciousness. Simply stated, you should never receive gifts that have been obtained illegally or from questionable means. Righteousness and unrighteousness cannot be mixed: *"A little leaven leavens the whole lump"* (Galatians 5:9 NKJ). Gifts are legitimate and should be seen as favor from God!

Another means by which money comes to the Believer is by inheritance. This is another form of a gift! Compensation for legitimate damages is another way to receive money. Now there is a caution: There are so many "slip and fall" incidences and our society has become very litigious. Never participate in schemes to defraud anyone—even if it is a company. Last, investments will produce prosperity. These are all of the ways that God will manifest prosperity in your life! As your financial prosperity appears, you must commit to use it biblically.

There are six ways to use money righteously (biblically):

1. Supporting the Kingdom of God. This includes tithes, offerings, and any sacrificial giving.
2. Paying your taxes. This is biblical and should be done without reservation.
3. Paying your debts. This reflects on your integrity.
4. Providing for your family.
5. Giving to the poor.
6. Saving to accumulate wealth.

God has not designed you to live from paycheck to paycheck! The simple fact is that when you have more, you can do more! God wants you financially prosperous so that you can represent Him in the earth! Receive this truth into your life and expect financial prosperity as a part of your Maximized Life!

Day 20 - Prosperity Explained

Maximized Prayer:

Father, financial prosperity is Your will for the Believer. I vow to live righteously so that I may receive financial prosperity. When my prosperity manifests, I will use it righteously and bring glory to You. In Jesus' name, Amen.

Maximizing Moments:

Answer the questions from today's lesson:

How do you handle the money you possess now?

How far will you go to get money?

How will you handle money when you have abundance?

Maximizing Mantra:

I confess that God is able to send wealth to me and through me to accomplish HIS will in the earth.

Revelation of Prosperity

NOTES

DAY 21 – PROSPERITY WITH PURPOSE

*"But remember the Lord your God!
It is He who gives you the power to become rich,
keeping the agreement He promised to your ancestors, as it is today."*
Deuteronomy 8:18 (NCV)

It is not enough to be able to dispel the myths about prosperity. God wants to bless His children abundantly for a reason! As you have already seen, God is a God of purpose and everything He does is on purpose for a purpose! The same is true for financial prosperity.

Prosperity is not about the accumulation of possessions to provide personal enjoyment. The Maximized Life includes biblical prosperity where all needs—natural, spiritual, and emotional—are met as a result of righteous, disciplined decision-making that brings the will of God to pass in your life. The wrong pursuit of prosperity delays the Maximized Life.

The wrong pursuit is ***Perverted Prosperity***. Perverted prosperity is all about things! It's all about clothing labels, models of cars, posh dwellings, the right zip codes, impressing people, and selfish ambition. Perverted prosperity is characterized by greed and selfishness. This perversion causes one to do anything for money and ignore the legitimate purpose for which money is given!

Purposeful Prosperity, on the other hand, is all about pleasing God! As a Maximizer, you realize that God is the source of your prosperity—at whatever level you are! As today's reading indicates, God *"gives you the power to become rich."* So God orchestrates bringing wealth into your life. Because God is the author of your prosperity, He has the right to establish the purpose for it and He has! He expects you to use your resources—that which He has entrusted to you—to fulfill His will in the earth.

So what is God's will concerning prosperity? To bless His children and expand His kingdom. God is a good God and He is a good Father: *"Whatever is good and perfect comes down to us from God our Father, who created all the lights in the heavens. He never changes or casts a shifting shadow"* (James 1:17 NLT). God authors good in our lives because He is a good Father: *"So I say to you, ask, and it will be given to you; seek, and you will find; knock, and it will be opened to you. For everyone who asks receives, and he who seeks finds, and to him who knocks it will be opened. If a son asks for bread from any father among you, will he give him a stone? Or if he asks for a fish, will he give him a serpent instead of a fish? Or if he asks for an egg, will he offer him a scorpion? If you then, being evil, know how to give good gifts to your children, how much more will your heavenly Father give the Holy Spirit to those who ask Him"* (Luke 11:9-13 NKJ).

Think of it this way: If your children obeyed you in all that you directed them and a need surfaced in their lives, would you neglect them? Of course not! You would give them whatever they needed! So, if this comes naturally to us, how much more for God? In fact, He is the model Father! (That is why the model prayer opens acknowledging Him as Father.) God is good to His children. God wants you blessed because, if you are not blessed, you cannot be a blessing.

God made a promise to Abraham: *"The Lord had said to Abram, 'Leave your native country, your relatives, and your father's family, and go to the land that I will show you. I will make you into a great nation. I will bless you and make you famous, and you will be a blessing to others. I will bless those who bless you and curse those who treat you with contempt. All the families on earth will be blessed through you'"* (Genesis 12:1-3 NLT). This is the agreement that God references

Day 21 - Prosperity with Purpose

in your reading today. Your modern-day prosperity is God making good on the promise He made to Abraham. And you have a right to this promise as a Believer: *"You belong to Christ, so you are Abraham's descendants. You will inherit all of God's blessings because of the promise He made to Abraham"* (Galatians 3:29 NCV). And God takes *"pleasure in the prosperity of His servant"* (Psalm 35:27 NKJ).

How can you be a blessing to someone else if you are not blessed? God's purposes for prosperity are fulfilled in your giving to His Kingdom and being a blessing to others. God loves people and He wants them in relationship with Him. When your prosperity advances the Kingdom of God, you are responsible for transformation in the lives of people. God does not want anyone to be lost: *"The Lord is not slack concerning his promise, as some men count slackness; but is longsuffering to us-ward, not willing that any should perish, but that all should come to repentance"* (2 Peter 3:9 KJV).

To spread the Gospel, it takes resources. So, in addition to you being blessed, God wants people saved! Your prosperity should translate into souls for the Kingdom of God. Never take this lightly! God wants you to walk in abundance so that whenever there is a need, His children will have ready resources. God loves people and the Maximizer loves people as well: *"For God so loved the world, that he gave his only begotten Son, that whosoever believeth in him should not perish, but have everlasting life"* (John 3:16 NLT). Your heart's desire has to be to see people brought into the knowledge of God! You will then dedicate your resources to fulfilling God's purposes.

Now you may be wondering, "What about me? If all my resources go to God's Kingdom, what happens to me and my family?" Fair question! Here is what you should know: When water

Revelation of Prosperity

flows through a pipe, the pipe gets wet, too! As prosperity flows through your hands, you will be able to keep portions of it. You will be able to live the life of abundance because quality of life is possessed through giving. You will start to measure your life by your giving! Prosperity with purpose is about your heart's desire to please God with everything that He puts into your hands. When God sees that your heart is right towards Him and prosperity, you will walk in more than you could ever imagine! Always keep purpose with prosperity and you will never lose!

Maximized Meditation/Prayer:

Father, I accept your priorities for prosperity! I want to be a distribution center for the Kingdom of God. What you put into my hands will be used obediently to advance Your Kingdom. In Jesus' name, Amen.

Maximizing Moments:

Time to examine your heart: What would you do if you were expecting a financial blessing and you had made plans to spend it, however, God instructs you to give all of it away? What would you do? (Be honest. God knows the truth!)

Maximizing Mantra:

I am blessed to be a blessing!

DAY 22 – STRATEGIES FOR PROSPERITY

*"Save now, I pray, O LORD;
O LORD, I pray, send now prosperity."*
Psalm 118:25 (NKJ)

Now that you understand what prosperity is and why God wants you to prosper, all you need are strategies that will lead you to the prosperity God has planned! Today and tomorrow you will be presented with twelve (12) proven strategies to bring you into abundance.

Don't despise your small beginnings. Your starting point will not limit you. It is just that: a starting point! You have what you have because God has surveyed your present ability and has given you enough to demonstrate that you can be trusted with more: *"Does anyone dare despise this day of small beginnings? They'll change their tune when they see Zerubbabel setting the last stone in place"* (Zechariah 4:10 NLT)! It's how you finish that matters most! And, as a Maximizer, you will finish well—in a state of prosperity!

As you saw yesterday, God rejoices when the agreement is kept and things are fulfilled according to His destiny plan. You see, even though the beginnings may be small, they will not remain that way as long as you are found a good steward over your present circumstances. How you operate with what you currently have will prepare you for more. In the Parable of the Talents, you learned an important principle that should encourage you: *"The master was full of praise. ' Well done, my good and faithful servant. You have been faithful in handling this small amount, so now I will give you many more responsibilities. Let's celebrate together'"* (Matthew 25:21 NLT). Show yourself faithful with what you have and God will give you more!

Revelation of Prosperity

Become a consistent tither. Your prosperity covenant is established through the tithe. Tithing establishes your partnership with God: *"Begin by being honest. Do honest people rob God? But you rob me day after day. You ask, 'How have we robbed you?' The tithe and the offering—that's how! And now you're under a curse—the whole lot of you—because you're robbing me. Bring your full tithe to the Temple treasury so there will be ample provisions in my Temple. Test me in this and see if I don't open up heaven itself to you and pour out blessings beyond your wildest dreams"* (Malachi 3:8-10 MSG). You cannot steal from God and expect prosperity. By tithing, you demonstrate that God can trust you.

Tithing—giving 10% of your income to the work of God—is one of the best guarantees of prosperity ever known. Many of the world's richest individuals and most successful people have been devout tithers. By tithing consistently, you too can put into motion God's universal plan, bringing you into continual abundance. (Later on your journey, you will learn more about tithes and offerings.)

Plant targeted offerings (seed) against needs and desires. God does not respond to need; He responds to seed! When you plant financial seed against a need, God is invited to intervene. Throughout the Bible, needs were addressed with an offering to God. When Israel was facing a severe plague, David sought to stop it by giving an offering to the Lord. What David did in principle is what we should do. Bring an offering to give to the Lord for the need you have in your life. Target seed to meet needs. According to 2 Corinthians 9:7-8, when you give, God releases a grace (favor) on your life to bring you into the all-sufficiency He has for you! (You will learn more about offerings—sowing seed—in about 14 days.)

Day 22 - Strategies for Prosperity

Confess the Word of God on financial increase daily. When you confess (speak in agreement with God's Word), you release God's power to help you. The confession component of the faith process keeps you from using your mouth as a confirming witness with the devil. Your mind may become beset with thoughts of poverty and thoughts of prosperity, but what you say will confirm or deny His will for your life. If you speak in agreement with thoughts of poverty (which come from the devil), you will reject the Maximized Life. Your words are life! Speak words of prosperity over your life and you will see it manifest. (There is a Prosperity Confession in the Additional Resources Section.)

Listen to prosperity tapes on a daily basis. You were created to respond to repetitive information. A truth is established in this way: *"So then faith cometh by hearing, and hearing by the word of God"* (Romans 10:17 NKJ). Your faith is ignited when you hear the Word of God taught. Your faith will increase to obey God and do the things necessary to bring about change in your life. By listening to the Word of God, you protect your ears, which are the gateway to your heart. You are programming your thought life to think increase: Expect to increase.

Spend time meditating on increase. Meditation is a divine strategy to recondition your mind. As you continually practice this discipline, you will remove the boundaries that society and others have placed on you. Before you picked up this book, you were in your comfort zone. You were comfortable right where you were. As you have read, day after day, your boundaries have been pushed and you have begun to expand your capacity to believe God for more. The Word of God instead of the expectations of others will soon reset your boundaries. You should dedicate time daily to meditate on increase!

Meditation is seeing yourself on the canvas of your imagination in possession of what you desired that is in agreement with God's Word and praising Him in advance for it (Psalm 1:1-3).

That's it for today! You are making good progress! You have received foundational strategies that will lead you to prosperity. However, you have only skimmed the surface. For the rest of the Maximized Life Journey, you will gain a greater understanding of why these strategies are important and how they work. Even with your limited knowledge, begin to put these strategies into practice. You will experience the benefits; and, once you gain more knowledge, you will expect even more!

Maximized Prayer:
>Father, I have increase on my mind. I covenant to put into practice what I have learned today so that I can walk in Your plan for my life. Lord, send prosperity now! In Jesus' name, Amen.

Maximizing Moments:
>Where you are is a starting point. What is your prosperity dream for the future? (Write it down.)
>
>Are you a consistent giver (tithes and offerings)?
>
>Are your thoughts governed by expectations of hard times and financial struggle or big dreams for the future?

Maximizing Mantra:
>I am faithful with what I have and am qualified for more!

DAY 23 – PROSPERING ON PURPOSE

*"Their houses brim with wealth
And a generosity that never runs dry."*
Psalm 112:3 (MSG)

You are well on your way to prosperity! And this is just what those who do not believe need to see. It is time for the Body of Christ to stand up and walk in the abundance that God has designed. The world will never take the Church seriously as long as everything it does is second class. When you walk in your covenant of prosperity, you will draw the attention of people around you. You should use those occasions to glorify what God has done in and through you: *"This is the Lord's doing, and it is wonderful to see"* (Psalm 118:23 NLT).

As a result of what you are learning, wealth will be in your house; and even your children's children will be blessed! Let's continue learning strategies for prosperity.

Keep your heart clean. The condition of your heart will determine the amount of time it takes for your prosperity to manifest. There is a preappointed time for your harvest, but you as the farmer must be ready for it. As you saw yesterday, daily meditation is a part of keeping your heart pure. If you allow pollution to enter your heart through the absence of meditation, it will stifle your productivity and frustrate your path to prosperity: *"But they start worrying about the needs of this life. They are fooled by the desire to get rich and to have all kinds of other things. So the message gets choked out, and they never produce anything"* (Mark 4:19 CEV). Your righteous resolve will weaken if you are not careful.

You must also watch out for strife because it will kill your faith fruit! Strife is dangerous: *"The beginning of strife is as when water first trickles [from a crack in a dam]; therefore stop contention before it becomes worse and quarreling breaks out"* (Proverbs 17:14 AMP). Where strife is present, all manner of evil is present and your heart will become polluted. Strife, particularly in a marriage partnership, delays manifestations because it breaks the agreement in the relationship.

In addition to strife, jealousy is to be avoided: *"You are still not spiritual, because there is jealousy and quarreling among you, and this shows that you are not spiritual. You are acting like people of the world"* (1 Corinthians 3:3 NCV). The prodigal son's brother (Luke 15:25-32) is a prime example of this. He missed out on the joy of being in the father's house because he was jealous of his brother's recognition. Jealousy is the evil premonition born out of comparison that creates internal pain and discomfort when you see others being blessed. When jealousy and strife are present, you become a ticking time bomb and your harvest will be withheld from you!

Identify and eliminate wealth thieves. Greed is a thief because it destroys the divine purpose of money and cancels the enjoyment factor of prosperity. It is the insatiable, covetous desire for abundance as an end unto itself. It perverts the purpose of God. Though you are on your way to increase, you are not given permission to live beyond your means. This greed will cause extreme debt; and, debt mismanagement is inevitable. When prosperity arrives, it only fills up an ever-growing deficit because of the debt mismanagement.

Another wealth thief is inefficient tax strategies. The Scripture is clear that we are to pay our taxes. Evading taxes is illegal and biblically immoral! Prolonged tax evasion positions you to put at risk all that God wants to do in your life! All of these will steal your wealth and rob you of the prosperity God so eagerly wants to give you! Identify these thieves in your own life and eliminate them immediately.

See yourself as an avenue of blessings for others. There is great benefit in serving! At whatever level you are right now, begin to be an avenue of blessing. Find ways to help and bless others: *"And anyone who gives you a cup of water in my name, just because you belong to me, will surely be rewarded"* (Mark 9:41 CEV). God will always honor those who see themselves as an avenue of blessings for others. Many people make promises to be generous when they reach a certain level. However, you should prove yourself faithful with what you have now; then, you will get to the place of abundance. If God cannot trust you to be a blessing now, He will not have a justifiable reason to give you more. God needs to see your faithfulness now in order to take you to your wealthy place. Service in the Kingdom of God must be a priority.

Begin to pay yourself each paycheck. Everything that comes into your hands is not to be spent! You should break the habit of spending everything that comes in; and, certainly, you should stop overspending! It is not God's desire for you to live from paycheck to paycheck. God is a God of more than enough and He desires that you have more than enough. If you spend everything that comes into your hand, you will never arrive at the place of abundance. Each time you receive increase, in addition to giving, you should save. It may be a small amount at the beginning, but do not accept the lie from the devil that says you should wait until you have more to save. Start now! Saving requires discipline. You will recall that the definition for discipline is enforced obedience. Make yourself save!

Live in daily expectation for increase and the divine opportunity to surface. Are you expecting to be blessed? Or do you face each day with dread? As a Maximizer, you should awaken each day with renewed expectation that God will do *"exceedingly abundantly above all that"* you could ask or think (Ephesians 3:20 NKJ). *"Blessed be the Lord, Who daily loads us with benefits"* (Psalm 68:19 NKJ). God can never operate above your expectations. Raise you expectations that God will increase you more and more and more and more (Psalm 115:14)! You should expect to be loaded with benefits daily!

Last, *be courageous and bold enough to obey God.* We talked about obedience a few days ago. Your road to prosperity will follow every obedient act! When you, as an act of your will, choose to obey God, it provokes prosperity. When you make a natural decision to do something in your life, and with your life, that will glorify God, you trigger the supernatural power of God and the grace of God to bring it to pass. So, then, acceptance from God must be your only priority. You should only be concerned about how God views you and no one else. When you come to this understanding, you will begin to make bold actions at the not-knowing level. This is faith in action!

Now you have the strategies to produce prosperity in your life. Practice them daily and see the benefits; you are on the road to prosperity!

Day 23 - Prospering on Purpose

Maximized Prayer:
Father, I pray for courage! Courage to obey You in all things so that I am found faithful. I bring into captivity every thought against Your prosperity plan for my life. In Jesus' name, Amen.

Maximizing Moments:
Do you have a financial plan including a budget?

Are you living paycheck to paycheck?

How will you manage the prosperity God sends? (You should have a plan now.)

Maximizing Mantra:
Daily, God loads me with benefits!

NOTES

DAY 24 – MASTERING THE MECHANICS

"But be sure that everything is done properly and in order."
1 Corinthians 14:40 (NLT)

The next several days will take your journey to a whole new level! You are going to be exposed to proven principles for planning and problem solving. These principles are time tested and work!

Based upon what you have learned earlier, here's is the definition of a problem: A problem is a temporary interruption in a plan that produces discomfort, discouragement, disagreements, or distress that must be overcome so that purposes and objectives will be realized. The source of these various problems may be spiritual, which must be addressed; but the natural effect must be handled.

Over the next 2 days, you will learn ten (10) steps, which will revolutionize your problem-solving ability and set the stage for proactive planning for your Maximized Life.

The first step in problem solving is cultivating a solution-oriented mentality. You may recall the story of Chicken Little, who saw doom and destruction around every corner. The seemingly small indicators sent Chicken Little on a rampage of worry and fear. Is this an accurate assessment of how you approach problems? There is no problem that you can face for which God has not already prepared a solution.

Let's look at 1 Corinthians 10:13 in its entirety: *"For no temptation (no trial regarded as enticing to sin), [no matter how it comes or where it leads] has overtaken you and laid hold on you that is not common to man [that is, no temptation or trial has come to you that is beyond human resistance and that is not adjusted and adapted and belonging to human experience, and such as man can bear]. But*

Responsibility for Planning

God is faithful [to His Word and to His compassionate nature], and He [can be trusted] not to let you be tempted and tried and assayed beyond your ability and strength of resistance and power to endure, but with the temptation He will [always] also provide the way out (the means of escape to a landing place), that you may be capable and strong and powerful to bear up under it patiently" (AMP).

You cannot face a problem for which God hasn't already provided an answer. Thus, when you embarked upon the Maximized Life Journey, you need to know that God has your solution! There is a way out of wherever you are. Regardless of the situation you face, God has a way of escape already designed.

Always be on the lookout for solutions. If you are solution oriented, you will not be problem oriented. What you focus on will be magnified in your life. If you focus on the problem, it will become so large that it will appear to be bigger than God. However, when you focus on the solutions (or seek for solutions), you will be drawn to new avenues of possibilities that may have been hidden. Know that there is a solution for whatever you are facing.

Second, don't procrastinate! When the problem appears, you must demonstrate intentionality in your response. We have heard it said, "He who hesitates is lost." Be proactive, not reckless or premature. Establish a sense of urgency. When urgency is present, it will marshal unexpected resources to aid you. If there are others involved, it is good to involve them early in the process of solving the problem. If you sense paralysis setting in, do something intentional to move forward. Problems left unchecked will engulf your life. Remember, God has your solution and His wisdom can turn your negative situation into a positive one.

Day 24 - Mastering the Mechanics

Third, eliminate the threat environment. Problems arise as threats, and they come with a voice and an environment. You must diffuse the threat so that you are not intimidated. It may be hostile interactions with a spouse or child. It may be tensions with a co-worker. It may be impending financial calamity. Each of these scenarios carries with it a threat and a voice. Persistent arguing and nagging phone calls set the stage for exponential problems! Your mindset should always be to disarm environments so that you are not dominated by the problem.

You may recall what happened when the disciples were on the boat and an unexpected storm arose: *"Late that day he said to them, 'Let's go across to the other side.' They took him in the boat as he was. Other boats came along. A huge storm came up. Waves poured into the boat, threatening to sink it. And Jesus was in the stern, head on a pillow, sleeping! They roused him, saying, 'Teacher, is it nothing to you that we're going down?' Awake now, he told the wind to pipe down and said to the sea, 'Quiet! Settle down!' The wind ran out of breath; the sea became smooth as glass. Jesus reprimanded the disciples: 'Why are you such cowards? Don't you have any faith at all'"* (Mark 4:35-39 MSG)? The disciples panicked and even went to chastise Jesus for His seeming disinterest. Jesus, a perfect example of reducing the threat environment, simply spoke to the storm and it obeyed Him. He could have joined the disciples in their fear-filled behavior, but Jesus knew that would not solve the problem. Your faith-filled response to problems will cause situations to be disarmed, and it will even calm others around you. At this disarming stage, do not become emotional or follow your feelings. You will give the problem authority over you if you respond by feelings.

Responsibility for Planning

As you know, you have been encouraged to be reflective throughout this journey. *Fourth, before you can proceed with problem solving, you will need to analyze and identify the problem.* There are many sources to the problems we face. They are all not caused by the devil: *"A curse you don't deserve will take wings and fly away like a sparrow or a swallow"* (Proverbs 26:2 CEV). There is a reason for what you are going through. This analytical stage will give you the ability to properly discern what the problem is and to identify the source(s) of the problem. This exercise is not designed to bring condemnation but clarity. If you know what and why, then you can effectively plan.

Honesty and transparency should be evident at this step. Don't be afraid to document all of your findings. Answer questions like, "What is the source of this problem?" "Is the source satan, the Sovereign, or self?" The source of the problem will determine the steps necessary to resolve the problem. You cannot move forward until the real issues are outlined and understood. As painful as it may feel, this step will maximize the learning you gain from your current situation.

The fifth step, which is very closely related to the fourth, is documenting the contributing factors. Because there is a cause for everything, you should list all the variables that have led to your current situation. These variables may also include people. Who or what is involved in your current problems? At this stage, you will actually be creating action steps towards your solution. There may be immediate consequences that you can forestall by identifying contributing factors early in the process. There may even be some midcourse corrections, which can be taken immediately to lessen the impact of your current problem. All of this should be documented.

This is just the beginning. There are five (5) more steps that we will discuss tomorrow. But you can start today applying these five (5) principles that enable you to bring your problems under control. You will see that problems are manageable, with the help of God.

Maximized Prayer:
Father, give me the courage to face the problems in my life and the wisdom to create a plan. In Jesus' name, Amen.

Maximizing Moments:
Begin to chart a course to solve the problems in your life by creating your plan.

Maximizing Mantra:
I possess the wisdom to solve problems.

NOTES

Day 25 – Managing Your Problems

"Such a large crowd of witnesses is all around us! So we must get rid of everything that slows us down, especially the sin that just won't let go. And we must be determined to run the race that is ahead of us."
Hebrews 12:1 (CEV)

As you start today, be encouraged! Up to this point, you have been identifying problems and their sources. Before you complete the last five (5) steps, remain hopeful. It is easy to think of quitting once you confront the problem and its causes. However, there is a lot at stake; please don't forget that.

So what is at stake if you don't keep going? First, when you don't learn a lesson that you are supposed to learn, you are doomed to repeat it. Let it not be said of you, *"Ever learning, and never able to come to the knowledge of the truth"* (2 Timothy 3:7 KJV). You will continue to travel on the same pathway experiencing déjà vu moments when problems are not adequately solved.

Next, when you abdicate your responsibility to solve problems, you are walking in disobedience to God's will for your life. And, if you want the best that God has to offer, you must examine your life and where it is going: *"If you are willing and obedient, You shall eat the good of the land"* (Isaiah 1:19 NKJ). Your Maximized Life Journey will never come to completion if you run from problems.

Let's be honest. Some of the problems you are facing are of your own making. (It's hard to hear, but it is helpful for your future.) To err and refuse correction is the mark of the unwise and foolish. Paul told the church in Corinth, *"A man ought to examine himself before he eats of the bread and drinks of the cup"* (1 Corinthians 11:28 NIV). Self-examination is a part of the Christian life. You should regularly examine yourself to see if there are attitudes and behaviors that are hindering your growth. You may not like what you find, but this is

Responsibility for Planning

the beginning of your journey to change when you can honestly identify where you are and what has caused you to be there.

When you read Deuteronomy 30:19, you saw that your decision to "choose life" today will impact the lives of others who follow you. The example you leave for others will impact their lives more than all your speeches. Your diligent choices today will position those who follow you to be blessed.

Moreover, if you side-step problem solving in your life, you may run the risk that God will cancel your assignment and erase the memory of your participation. How sad it would be to see others assume the place that God had established for you simply because you refused to change? There is a lot at stake in this Maximized Life Journey.

So let's return to the action steps.

The sixth step is the research and exploration step. Who can help solve this problem? Are there others who have been in similar situations? How did they handle what you are going through? Assess your strengths, weaknesses, threats, and opportunities. Remember to document. What are all of the options available to you? Be exhaustive! Write this all down. One of your most valuable tools in problem solving is your pen! Spend time refining your list and aligning it with your specific problem. You will begin to see next steps emerge that you can take.

Next, be transparent enough to share your thoughts with responsible others. Some problem solving is a team sport! This team will also serve as an accountability group throughout the process: *"Without good direction, people lose their way; the more wise counsel you follow, the better your chances"* (Proverbs 11:14 MSG). This solutions team

Day 25 - Managing Your Problems

can assist you in refining solutions and action steps. As you chart a course to the future, don't be married to one idea over another. There are no bad ideas. Your team may be your spouse, family members, mentor, or friends. Allow their wisdom to assist you in shaping a path for your Maximized Life Journey.

After you have assembled your team and completed your research, then you should write out a plan of action. Your plan should be detailed and contain all that you have learned from the previous steps. God can help you if you have a plan: *"A man's heart plans his way, But the LORD directs his steps"* (Proverbs 16:9 NKJ). It bears repeating: Your plan should be written in detail. And it should be rehearsed regularly. You will live in the future; you might as well live in a future that you planned: *"Good planning and hard work lead to prosperity, but hasty shortcuts lead to poverty"* (Proverbs 21:5 MSG). The absence of a real plan will end in more problems and lack. It is also good at this stage to document new guidelines and procedures that you need to implement to guard against the problem recurring. There may need to be boundaries established or decisions memorialized. Whatever they are, *write them down*!

Once your plan is finished and you are implementing it, it is time for reflection. Capture the lessons that you have learned. Categorize them as "Never again will I..." and "From now on, I will...." This is the personal growth component that you cannot skip. Your professional and personal growth depends on it. It is okay to confront your weaknesses. As you manage them, you will see real growth and begin to accelerate towards your destiny.

Last, choose to move forward without carrying emotional baggage. Scars are a part of problems. Once you have spent your reflection time, you must close the door on the past and the process. The role

Responsibility for Planning

that people have played in either the problem or the problem solving may have caused offenses. Release them quickly. You may also need to forgive yourself for the shortcomings that produced the problems. Because you have a plan, you have a way forward.

Do not carry old emotions into a new situation. You may need to spend more time renewing your mind to shed all the sins and weights, which are surrounding you (Hebrews 12:1). Your decisions to live offense-free and leave emotional baggage will grant you the agility to maneuver towards your future. It's time to look forward, not back. Your choice to rejoice will keep your emotions in check.

With these ten (10) steps, you have a proven problem-solving regimen that can transform your minimal life to a Maximized Life!

Maximized Prayer:
Father, I need Your strength to master this process so that I do not falter. I must complete this journey. In Jesus' name, Amen.

Maximizing Moments:
Continue the creation of your problem-solving plan.

Maximizing Mantra:
I solve problems and I am rewarded!

DAY 26 – IT'S NOT GOD'S FAULT

"Whatever is good and perfect comes down to us from God our Father, who created all the lights in the heavens. He never changes or casts a shifting shadow."
James 1:17 (NLT)

Now that you are equipped to solve the problems you face, you need a clear understanding of the source of your problems. Too often people feel compelled to blame someone for their situation in life. They blame spouses, they may blame the lack of academic attainment, or they may even blame God!

If you are going to be a Maximizer, it will require that you have an unshakable theology about who is the cause of the problems in your life. If you think God is against you or is the author of the challenges you face, it will be difficult for you to muster the strength to plan for the future. And you will then sink into a lethargic mindset that says, "Whatever the Lord wants will just come to pass."

Today's verse of Scripture identifies the heart of God! God is the Author of only good things in your life! You may ask, "How can this be?" In the face of terror plots, sinking retirements, failing marriages, rampant unemployment and the inexplicable loss of loved ones, an overriding question emerges, "Where is God in all this?"

As you have already seen, adversity is a part of the human experience: *"Many evils confront the [consistently] righteous, but the Lord delivers him out of them all"* (Psalm 34:19 AMP). But God has given us the ability to overcome them all: *"I am grateful that God always makes it possible for Christ to lead us to victory. God also helps us spread the knowledge about Christ everywhere, and this knowledge is like the smell of perfume"* (2 Corinthians 2:14 CEV).

Responsibility for Planning

There are several reasons for adversity in your life: human error, challenges of the time, satanic attack, or the call of God. As you saw earlier, you often play a role in the challenges that you face. It may be from ignorance that you commit a human error that complicates your life. Sometimes, though, adversities come just because of the times. In the current climate, there is a lot of talk of recession and depression. As a result, certain responses are triggered in society. We also understand that there is an enemy who opposes everything that you seek to accomplish. So some of your adversities are orchestrated by evil forces: *"A thief comes only to rob, kill, and destroy"* (John 10:10 CEV). Last, because God has something special that He wants you to complete, there may be resistance that you face.

Regardless of the reason for the challenges, God does not author evil in anyone's life! It is God's will for you to overcome everything: *"For whatsoever is born of God overcometh the world: and this is the victory that overcometh the world, even our faith"* (1 John 5:4 KJV).

But wait! Job stated emphatically, and you may have heard it preached in a church, *"The LORD gave, and the LORD hath taken away; blessed be the name of the LORD"* (Job 1:21 KJV). Job's words are correct from his point of view, but they are not true! Imagine if a famous speaker, in his ignorance, said that there is no city called Dallas in the state of Texas. The newspaper reports that this famous person made this statement. The newspaper reports accurately but the statement, though accurately reported, is not true! You know Job's statement is not true because, as you read in the earlier verses, satan desired for the hedge of protection to be lifted from Job. (Satan thought that Job only served God when He had all the evidence of blessings!) The devil is the antagonist and accuser of God's people!

Day 26 - It's Not God's Fault

So how did the hedge of protection come down around Job? Look at what he states later: *"The worst of my fears has come true, what I've dreaded most has happened"* (Job 3:25 MSG). Job possessed fear and that fear gave satan an open door to attack him. The Bible warns us, *"Leave no [such] room or foothold for the devil [give no opportunity to him]"* (Ephesians 4:7 AMP). The devil will always exploit any space that you give him. If you give him an inch, he will take a mile! He will not stop until he destroys you!

God's foreknowledge of a situation does not make Him responsible for it. In a like manner, you cannot blame the weather person because they predict that a hurricane is coming. Yes, God is all knowing. However, just because God knows about it and sees it, God cannot violate the order that He has established on the earth. God will allow what you permit: *"And I will give you the keys of the Kingdom of Heaven. Whatever you forbid on earth will be forbidden in heaven, and whatever you permit on earth will be permitted in heaven"* (Matthew 16:19 NLT). God only permits what you give authority to take place in your life!

When you read the account of Paul's "thorn in the flesh," many have misconstrued this story to suggest that God sent an attack on Paul to keep him humble. However, Paul is very clear about the source of the attack: *"One of Satan's angels was sent to make me suffer terribly, so that I would not feel too proud. Three times I begged the Lord to make this suffering go away. But he replied, 'My kindness is all you need. My power is strongest when you are weak.' So if Christ keeps giving me his power, I will gladly brag about how weak I am"* (2 Corinthians 12:7-9 CEV).

Notice that God tells Paul that He has been given the power to handle whatever the devil is throwing at him! God will always allow

Responsibility for Planning

what you allow. And God will disallow any and everything that you disallow! The power has been given to you! You are in control of your future! You are not a victim at the hands of God!

God always wants you to win and He has dispatched His power to help you: *"For I can do everything through Christ, who gives me strength"* (Philippians 4:13 NLT). How will God strengthen you? Paul prays, *"That he would grant you, according to the riches of his glory, to be strengthened with might by his Spirit in the inner man"* (Ephesians 3:16 KJV). God will strengthen you so that you will always win. You can always count on God's help as you move towards the Maximized Life.

But, you may ask, "What if God is trying to punish me for past bad decisions for which I feel guilty?" You are correct that, in extreme cases, God does bring judgment; but in those cases, God does not want it to happen: *"And I sought for a man among them, that should make up the hedge, and stand in the gap before me for the land, that I should not destroy it: but I found none"* (Ezekiel 22:30 KJV).

God did not want to bring judgment, but God could not find anyone who would intercede to reverse the judgment. But, please know, God would never kill you or anyone in your family because of your sins! As a Christian Believer, when you have committed a sin, you can ask for forgiveness and God will freely give it to you (1 John 1:9). God is long-suffering and His mercy endures forever.

So you can see that God is not to blame for the adversities that you are facing. But He will help you turn the situation around! When you blame God for the bad that has happened in your life, you limit God's ability to help you! You turn *against* God rather than turn *to* God. But when you turn to God, God will dispatch His

Day 26 – It's Not God's Fault

power to help turn any situation around. This is good news: *It's not God's fault!*

Maximized Prayer:
Father, You desire nothing more than to help me! You sent Jesus to rescue me and help me so that I can win in every area of my life. I receive this help daily to overcome every obstacle in my life. In Jesus' name, Amen!

Maximizing Moment:
In what areas have I mistakenly blamed God?

Repent for this and ask God to help you successfully complete your Maximized Life Journey.

Maximizing Mantra:
God's promise to me is abundant life, and I will not settle for anything less!

Responsibility for Planning

NOTES

DAY 27 – GET READY FOR FRESH FIRE

"But my horn shalt thou exalt like the horn of an unicorn:
I shall be anointed with fresh oil."
Psalm 92:10 (KJV)

For the Maximizer, there is a relentless pursuit of the plans and purposes of God! Fatigue, weariness, burnout and loss of passion should not describe your Maximized Life. Yet, with all that you must do and keep doing to stay on this journey, how do you ensure that you don't grow weary?

Well, God has designed a Helper for you Who will go with you through this Journey: *"I will ask the Father, and he will give you another Helper to be with you forever— the Spirit of truth. The world cannot accept him, because it does not see him or know him. But you know him, because he lives with you and he will be in you"* (John 14:16-17 NCV). This Helper (Advocate/Comforter) is the Holy Spirit. He was sent by God to help you accomplish all that God has assigned for you to do. You cannot achieve the purpose for which God created you without His help.

Since God has promised His children assistance on the journey, why are so many Believers giving up and walking away from the Maximized Life? Could it be that Believers have neglected the ministry of the Holy Spirit? Could it be that people in the church have ignored the Holy Spirit's role in their spiritual growth and development? Sadly, the answer to these questions is "Yes."

When you receive the Holy Spirit and are in constant fellowship with Him, you are less prone to become spiritually tired or burned out. Walking in the Spirit is a personal, private fellowship with the Holy Spirit that others may not see. However, the results of it are seen in the passion you have for living a life that pleases God.

Responsibility for Planning

When you realize that you have not given full attention to the day-to-day ministry of the Holy Spirit and repent for having ignored His presence, you will position yourself to experience the Fresh Fire Anointing! As you work to intentionally restore your fellowship with the Holy Spirit or establish a fellowship with Him, a refreshing will come over you like the times of refreshing in the Bible.

This Fresh Fire Anointing is a supernatural impartation that gives you the divine ability to accomplish things you could not accomplish on your own. When you walk in this power, you will not only have a restored passion but you will have four dimensions of power for abundant living released upon your life. The Fresh Fire Anointing manifests the power for holiness, power of hope, power for harvest and power for healing!

Fresh fire is a spiritual impartation born out of an intentionally cultivated relationship with the Holy Spirit that ignites or reignites a passion for God. Fresh fire replenishes the power of God in your life so that you can be an effective witness in this generation.

After the day of Pentecost, Peter spoke of a time of refreshing: *"Repent ye therefore, and be converted, that your sins may be blotted out, when the times of refreshing shall come from the presence of the Lord"* (Acts 3:19). He makes it clear that you can get tired spiritually and need to be refreshed. That is where many people are right now. Some are worn out because they have been doing some things they were not supposed to do. Others are frustrated and are about to faint because they have neglected the ministry of the day-to-day fellowship with Holy Spirit. Still others have reached their breaking point. They are living compromised lives because they lack

Day 27 - Get Ready for Fresh Fire

the knowledge to manifest His strength for holy living. The Word of God promises times of restoration and times of refreshing.

It is the will of God that you become a born-again Believer and receive the Holy. This is a simple but dynamic step. As Romans 10:9 teaches, when you accept that Jesus lived, that He died for your sins and that He was raised from the dead, you can be saved. Further, you are intentionally encouraged to cultivate a relationship with the Holy Spirit for the strength and power needed to pursue the Maximized Life!

The Fresh Fire Anointing brings a passion for God and the things of the kingdom of God. You will be excited about righteousness, holiness, church, your pastor's vision and ministry to others! You will never want to quit or give up on your Maximized Life!

"Whenever, though, they turn to face God as Moses did, God removes the veil and there they are—face-to-face! They suddenly recognize that God is a living, personal presence, not a piece of chiseled stone. And when God is personally present, a living Spirit, that old, constricting legislation is recognized as obsolete. We're free of it! All of us! Nothing between us and God, our faces shining with the brightness of his face. And so we are transfigured much like the Messiah, our lives gradually becoming brighter and more beautiful as God enters our lives and we become like him. Since God has so generously let us in on what he is doing, we're not about to throw up our hands and walk off the job just because we run into occasional hard times" (2 Corinthians 3:16-4:1 MSG).

Responsibility for Planning

Maximized Prayer:
Father, You have made the Holy Spirit available to me. I receive Him into my life and submit to His leading and direction. I commit to fellowship with Him daily so that I can walk in the Fresh Fire Anointing. In Jesus' name, Amen.

Maximizing Moments:
Have you intentionally invited the Holy Spirit to operate in your life?

Develop a resolve to depend upon the Holy Spirit every moment of every day.

Maximizing Mantra:
I walk in the Fresh Fire Anointing!

DAY 28 – OVERCOMING INFERIOR THOUGHTS

"For my thoughts are not your thoughts, neither are your ways my ways, saith the Lord. For as the heavens are higher than the earth, so are my ways higher than your ways and my thoughts than your thoughts." Isaiah 55:9 (NKJ)

Proverbs 23:7 begins by teaching you that you are as you think. It becomes very important, then, to manage how you think and what you are thinking about. To neglect your thought life can affect who you are and the purpose God has for your life. Moreover, incorrect thinking cripples decision making, retards faith, and keeps the victory at bay in life.

God told Israel to go and possess the land flowing with milk and honey. He never mentioned the other nations living in the same land, yet Israel was to go and get it. God also gives us great promises and, like Israel, we have to go and get them. For a while, Israel was having good success gaining territory. Then in Numbers 13:27-33, Israel declared an evil report, saying, *"We be not able to go up against the people; for they are stronger than we . . . we were in our own sight as grasshoppers and so we were in their sight."* God can never transcend your will. So, while God is capable and willing to honor His promise in your life, He cannot when we don't think properly.

Israel became intimidated because of their inferior thinking. If you recall the story, everything that God told them about the land was proven accurate: *"When they came to the valley of Eshcol, they cut down a branch with a single cluster of grapes so large that it took two of them to carry it on a pole between them! They also brought back samples of the pomegranates and figs"* (Numbers 13:23 NLT). Can you imagine? Grapes so large that one cluster required two people to carry it. This supersedes every expectation that Israel had. Yet, with

Responsibility for Planning

grapes in hand, they still could not overcome their inferior view of themselves!

In fact, Israel was delayed for 40 years as God waited for that entire generation to die so the new generation could accept the possibilities available to them. All because of their inferiority complex, they missed out on what God had in store for them. Thankfully, those who believed what God promised were able to enjoy the Promised Land. With Joshua and Caleb, Israel finally possessed the land of promise.

Another interesting aspect to this biblical account is that their inferior report was considered evil simply because it was not affirming God's report! This is a fact that you cannot escape. As you make your way through this journey, you must purpose in your heart to accept what God says about you and surrender everything that blocks your progress towards your Maximized Life!

Decision making is not solely based on facts, information, or opportunities at hand but is also based on how you have been trained to think. What you believe has a direct effect on how you see yourself. How you see yourself will affect the quality of the decisions that you make.

So how does God see you?

"The Lord will make you like the head and not like the tail; you will be on top and not on bottom." (Deuteronomy 28:13 NCV).

"But in all these things we are completely victorious through God who showed his love for us." (Romans 8:37 NCV)

God sees you victorious, on top of the world, living a Maximized Life! The challenge is for you to see yourself though God's eyes.

Day 28 - Overcoming Inferior Thoughts

One of the best decisions you can make as a Christian is to see yourself as God sees you. When you search the Scriptures, you find many promises that can fulfill you in life; but the biggest misconception is that God will bring it all to you and all you must do is wait for it patiently. The will of God and the promises of God are not automatic. As a Christian, you must be a willing participant in accepting what God has for you regardless of how big it appears or how overwhelming the situation looks.

When God told Moses to lead Israel out of Egyptian bondage, Moses limited his ability in his own mind. When God called Gideon to deliver Israel from the Midianites, his thinking limited him. When God used Deborah to speak to Barak, she too was not convinced in her own mind. When Esther was asked to save her people, she was inferior in her thinking. With these examples and the many others, you can see how easy it can be to think inferior; but in each of the examples, we also see the promise of God fulfilled because each person pushed beyond those initial thoughts to see God honor His Word in their lives. And in each case, He did. Thankfully, He'll do the same for you.

The goal, then, is to change how you think and what you're thinking about. You should no longer think like the world thinks in the futility of their thinking. Ephesians 4:18 says, *"They are darkened in their understanding and separated from the life of God because of the ignorance that is in them due to the hardening of their hearts"* (NKJ). What that means is you must deliberately get knowledge of God's will and open your heart to believe that what God says is possible for you. This further means you must change how you think if you're going to progress in life. Here are some scriptures that highlight the importance of changing your mindset:

Responsibility for Planning

"I beseech you therefore, brethren, by the mercies of God, that ye present your bodies a living sacrifice, wholly, acceptable unto God, which is your reasonable service. And be not conformed to this world; but be ye transformed by the renewing of your mind, that ye may prove what is that good, and acceptable, and perfect, will of God." (Romans 12:1-2 KJV)

"Finally, brethren, whatsoever things are true, whatsoever things are honest, whatsoever things are just, whatsoever things are pure, whatsoever things are lovely, whatsoever things are of good report; if there be any virtue, and if there be any praise, think on these things. Those things, which ye have both learned, and received, and heard, and seen in me, do: and the God of peace shall be with you." (Philippians 4:8-9 KJV)

Maximized Prayer:
Father, I see how you see me! I surrender my negative, inferior thoughts for your superior thoughts. I will begin the process of renewing my mind to overcome my inferior thoughts. In Jesus' name, Amen.

Maximizing Moments:
What are some inferior thoughts that you have of yourself?

Find Scripture to counteract those inferior images.

What would you accomplish if you knew that you couldn't fail?

Maximizing Mantra:
I am who God says I am!

Day 29 – Renewing Your Mind

"But we Have the Mind of Christ."
1 Corinthians 2:16 (NKJ)

What stands between you and the Maximized Life is better decision making. In order to improve the quality of your decisions, you must change your way of thinking. The Bible calls this renewing your mind.

Though you are a Believer and love God, when you came into the family of God, you brought with you old patterns of thinking and behavior that are hindrances to your growth and development. Most people never renew their minds; and, thus, they continue to experience less than God has promised. Not so for you because you are on a Journey to Maximize Your Life!

The next few days will be crucial in your journey because it is during this time that you will focus on the key component of your success: mental toughness. The Bible strongly exhorts the Believer to work at renewing the mind. You are responsible for the development and management of your thought life.

Here are some scriptures that underscore the biblical mandate to renew the mind:

"Beloved, I pray that you may prosper in all things and be in health, just as your soul prospers." (3 John 2 NKJ)

"Instead, let the Spirit renew your thoughts and attitudes." (Ephesians 4:23 NLT)

"We are human, but we don't wage war as humans do. We use God's mighty weapons, not worldly weapons, to knock down the strongholds of human reasoning and to destroy false arguments. We destroy every proud obstacle that keeps people from knowing God. We

Responsibility for Planning

capture their rebellious thoughts and teach them to obey Christ." (2 Corinthians 10:3-5 NLT)

It is crystal clear from these Scriptures that you, as a Believer, are responsible for participating in the transformation process and ongoing maintenance of your thought life. This is obligatory not optional.

Most people believe that renewing the mind is memorizing Scriptures. And, thus, they spend hours memorizing verse after verse so that the Bible is always on ready recall. However, memorizing Scripture and having Scripture govern our thought lives are two different things. When the Bible speaks of renewing the mind, it is talking about a transformation in our decision-making process. This means changing the fundamental thought patterns and beliefs that are programmed into you. Yes, programmed into you!

From birth until now, you have had a set of ideas and beliefs that have been adopted (intentionally and incidentally) as you have experienced life. Many of these, sadly, are not in line with God's best for your life. Your entrance into the Body of Christ does not change all of this inferior programming. Renewing the mind and conscious discipline are the two keys.

This is the development of mental toughness to make purposeful, accurate decisions on a consistent basis that produce a Maximized Life. To understand this process, you must understand the unique way that God created you to function.

1 Thessalonians 5:23 says that you are created as a tripartite being: spirit, soul, and body. You are a spirit who lives in a body who possesses a soul (mind). The soul has five (5) main components: mind, will, imagination, emotions, and intellect. The soul of a

Day 29 - Renewing Your Mind

person is what determines the unique personalities and characteristics of the person. The spirit is the eternal part and will exist after physical death (1 Thessalonians 5:23).

God chooses to work within the framework of how He created you to develop and mature. God understands that there are three parts to us, and He understands how each part functions in conjunction with the other parts. God has created us to accomplish His will in our lives. There is no shortcut to causing immediate transformation. It must come through a systematic process that has been designed to change or establish our thinking.

Our minds have three components to the mental complex: the conscious mind, the subconscious mind, and the conscience mind. These three work together in a dynamic way as our onboard computer to keep our lives on course.

The conscious mind handles the purposeful, conscious thoughts, and day-to-day decisions. The initial reasoning and logical thinking that require concentration and purposeful thinking are handled by this part of the mental complex. The subconscious, which is the autopilot of the conscious mind, has the responsibility to carry out automatically the finished work of the conscious mind.

When the conscious mind has thought through a process and has accepted certain norms and values as truth, from that moment on, the subconscious begins to handle decision making at a level that does not require much conscious thought at all. Your subconscious accesses your belief and value system and makes certain decisions automatically. This is a valuable asset for repetitious activities. (You will learn more about this in the coming days, but today you should familiarize yourself with the way God designed your mind to work.)

Responsibility for Planning

The last part of the mental complex is the conscience mind, which houses your belief system and value system. Your conscience is the foundation of your belief system. It is the reference point by which all things are judged. This is the heart of the mental complex for the decision-making process because it is here that all things are judged by a preconceived standard. As you experience life, the conscience acts as a central processing center for truth. The subconscious accesses information in the conscience and makes decisions on an ongoing basis without much thought.

This is a lot of material, but this information is crucial to your realizing the Maximized Life. Before tomorrow you should reread this to ensure that you understand the components of the mental complex.

Maximized Prayer:
> Father, You are a Wonder! I marvel at how You have made my mind! I submit to Your process of renewing my mind. In Jesus' name, Amen.

Maximizing Moments:
> Reread today's lesson and write out in your own words the definitions of conscious, subconscious, and conscience minds.

Maximizing Mantra:
> I am transformed by the renewing of my mind.

DAY 30 – MAXIMIZING YOUR MIND

"Throw off your old sinful nature and your former way of life, which is corrupted by lust and deception. Instead, let the Spirit renew your thoughts and attitudes."
Ephesians 4:22-23 (NLT)

Now that you have a sense of the way that God has created your mental complex to function, it is time to clearly understand how to renew your mind for maximum results. What you learn over the next several days is what being on this journey is all about: Maximizing Your Mind.

Remember, what you are going to learn over the next week is about more than memorizing Scripture for rapid recall. To have a renewed, or maximized, mind is to function in accordance with a new value and belief system. When Believers operate out of unregenerated minds, the Bible refers to them as carnal and as babes who are in need of milk! This cannot be you because you are on a Maximized Life Journey.

This is why prior to this journey you may have wrestled with the internal war of wanting to do the right thing and yet seemed to be locked into unrighteous misbehavior. The conscious mind houses the values and beliefs that govern our lives. It is like stacking or storing information on top of information: The more we learn, the more is stored.

Your subconscious has been programmed, or trained, to go to this storehouse of information to make decisions and give directions to the body. Think of it in this way: There are two sections in this conscience compartment, the Before Christ section and the After Christ section. For years, the subconscious has always accessed information from the Before Christ value section; and this old information is what is believed to be most reliable and a type of

Responsibility for Planning

perceived truth. When you came to the knowledge of Christ, you added biblical information on Christ-honoring behavior to the After Christ section. However, this information is not being accessed by the subconscious to automatically make decisions in agreement with it.

Here is where your effort comes in! In order to establish this information as reliable and, therefore, worthy of action, it will take many purposeful actions. Normally, after years of struggling, missteps, stress, and strain, the subconscious is retrained to access this information from the After Christ section; and it becomes easier to make righteous decisions. This is the hard way!

There is an orderly manner in which the mind functions; and, when properly understood, you can eliminate the years of struggle and accelerate the mind-renewing or maximizing process. You are going to learn how to effectively and systematically do just that: to retrain or reprogram the function of the subconscious so that it goes immediately to the After Christ section. At this point, the subconscious depends on the values and beliefs found in the After Christ section for reliable information and releases its dependence on the Before Christ values and beliefs.

In essence, to maximize or renew your mind is about transforming the operation of the mental complex so that all decisions are based on biblical truth and not unscriptural, experiential information that has been gathered over time, which may or may not be accurate. The transformation process is what is most challenging simply because of how God has designed your mind to function; you do not change easily. This is good because, otherwise, it would be difficult to maintain any kind of stable character or behavior if your standard of judgment could be easily manipulated.

Now much of what you are being presented is unfamiliar to you; and you may even be questioning if much of this is biblical since the word *subconscious* does not appear in the Bible. However, I want to encourage you to stay the course and read on! There are many words in the human lexicon that are not present in the Bible. For instance, the word *brain* is not in the Bible; yet we all know that we have one! In the same way, the mental complex, though not mentioned in the Bible, is very much real. The Scripture for today's reading expresses that there is more going on as the "*Spirit renews your thoughts and attitudes.*"

There is more to understand as you delve deeper into this transformation process. Are you ready to Maximize Your Mind?

Responsibility for Planning

Maximized Prayer:
Father, I reject every thought and belief that is not in line with Your Word and the plan that You have for my life! I ask the Holy Spirit to begin the renewing process of my mind as I learn more about meditation, In Jesus' name, Amen.

Maximizing Moments:
Here is a test of your subconscious:

What do you think about money?

Where did you learn to think this way about money? (This is just one example of how your subconscious governs your beliefs and values. This is true about how you see relationships, employment, etc.)

Maximizing Mantra:
I maximize my mind daily.

Day 31 – Shaping Your Conscience

"So with my mind I serve the Law of God, although my selfish desires make me serve the law of sin."
Romans 7:25 (CEV)

"Let your conscience be you guide!" You have heard this many times in life. And it is normally accepted as a positive statement. However, based on the understanding you are gaining about the mental complex, that may or may not be good advice. For, if your conscience has been formed from faulty or fraudulent information, your conscience, as it relates to spiritual things, is not trustworthy! If the conscience remains untrained and undeveloped, your conscience is most untrustworthy.

Now that you have become acquainted with how the mental complex functions, we can turn your attention to how your conscience is developed. Your belief and value systems, which are the basis for your decision-making, are shaped by four factors: social environment, credible authority figures, repetitious information, and personal experiences.

Your social environment helps shape what you believe about the world around you. It is not just your current day social environment but also the environment in which you were raised. In your developing years, you were totally innocent in your thinking; but as you began to develop, your social environment imposed certain perceived truths about life onto your value system. At that point, you locked into your decision-making process what was socially acceptable.

As it relates to credible authority figures, they teach you certain things about life and living that become part of your conscience. These authority figures are usually our parents, relatives, teachers,

Responsibility for Planning

and ministers whom we are told to respect and listen to. Credible authority figures affect how and what we choose to believe about life.

Then there is repetitious information. Your mind is designed to accept information that is fed to it on a consistent, repetitious basis. Whatever you hear over and over eventually makes its way into your thought process and affects the value system and decision process.

The billion-dollar advertising industry understands this. Madison Avenue firms understand that if you see or hear something repeatedly, it will alter or affect your thought process and possibly your belief system. Manufacturers of products spend billions of dollars with advertising firms to persuade you to think their products are the only ones you need. You are not changed by the first commercial that you see. But, over time, after you have been bombarded every 7 minutes with another commercial, you seem to lean towards purchasing that product, all of this without much explanation or conscious thought! When you see that product, regardless of its price in relation to other products, your belief system tells you this is the product you should purchase. Think about why you use certain products right now. You did not perform a market test or comparison shop. Most of the basic items you use today were introduced to you through repetitious information.

Last, your conscience is shaped and developed over time by personal experiences. Your personal experiences make the most potent and significant impact on your belief system. Here's an example: If you were asked along with a group of people to test out a brand new chair and the group was told that this chair can handle the weight of every person who sits on it. Then you were shown the manufacturer's calculations about the design and durability of the

Day 31 - Shaping Your Conscience

chair. The research team that designed the chair informed you of all the testing that was done to ensure that this chair could support the weight that was placed on it. Then you see person after person sit on the chair and have a great experience. You see larger people and smaller people sit comfortably on the chair. Now it's your turn. You approach the seat and sit on the chair like everyone else did; however, the chair collapses under your weight. Would you buy that chair? No! Because you would believe that the chair cannot handle your weight.

Your belief system would be influenced most by your personal experience rather than by what the manufacturer said. The statistics would be invalid for you, and even seeing other larger people sitting on the chair would be dispelled because of your personal experience. A personal experience is never at the mercy of the most profound argument! Your personal experience speaks loudest and will have the most impact on what you believe.

So, if you are going to change the inferior and Before Christ belief and value systems (which is your conscience), you must cooperate with the framework of these four factors. Now it actually makes more sense why God has insisted that Believers do certain things to develop a God-centered life.

As it relates to our environment, the Bible encourages Believers to control their environment and watch the company that they keep:

"And now I make one more appeal, my dear brothers and sisters. Watch out for people who cause divisions and upset people's faith by teaching things contrary to what you have been taught. Stay away from them." (Romans 16:17 NLT)

Responsibility for Planning

"Some people have gotten out of the habit of meeting for worship, but we must not do that. We should keep on encouraging each other, especially since you know that the day of the Lord's coming is getting closer." (Hebrews 10:25 CEV)

Understanding the impact credible authority has on us, the Bible establishes for the Believer the most reliable and dependable authority upon which to build one's life: the Word of God. Credible authority, for the Believer, is invested in God and His Word alone! God's Word must have preeminence over all things. It becomes the absolute standard by which all other information is judged:

"So Jesus said to those Jews who had believed in Him, If you abide in My word [hold fast to My teachings and live in accordance with them], you are truly My disciples. And you will know the Truth, and the Truth will set you free." (John 8:31-32 AMP)

"Heaven and earth shall pass away, but my words shall not pass away." (Matthew 24:35 KJV)

Honoring the repetitious information factor, the Word of God prescribes constant hearing of the Word of God, biblical meditation, the repetitious rehearsal of truth to children and a consistent prayer life:

"Write these commandments that I've given you today on your hearts. Get them inside of you and then get them inside your children. Talk about them wherever you are, sitting at home or walking in the street; talk about them from the time you get up in the morning to when you fall into bed at night. Tie them on your hands and foreheads as a reminder; inscribe them on the doorposts of your homes and on your city gates." (Deuteronomy 6:7-9 MSG)

Day 31 - Shaping Your Conscience

"So then faith comes by hearing, and hearing by the word of God." (Romans 10:17 NKJ)

"Blessed is the man Who walks not in the counsel of the ungodly, Nor stands in the path of sinners, Nor sits in the seat of the scornful; But his delight is in the law of the LORD, And in His law he meditates day and night. He shall be like a tree Planted by the rivers of water, That brings forth its fruit in its season, Whose leaf also shall not wither; And whatever he does shall prosper." (Psalm 1:1-3 NKJ)

And when it comes to experience, God encourages you to be steadfast through challenges while applying the principles of faith so that you will come through every one victoriously:

"We can rejoice, too, when we run into problems and trials, for we know that they help us develop endurance. And endurance develops strength of character, and character strengthens our confident hope of salvation." (Romans 5:3-4 NLT)

As you can see, God understands how He created your mental complex to work. The world's system is exploiting this information to brainwash our children and influence our decision-making. What would happen if you, as a Maximizer, leveraged this same information to build a strong spiritual foundation to your life? Simply put, you would be unstoppable!

Maximized Prayer:
> Father, You know more than I do about how you made me to operate. I will honor your process and renew my mind by reengineering my social environment to please You; acknowledging You and Your Word as my credible authority; repetitiously feeding myself Your Word; and standing firm in faith to see you deliver me from all my problems. I need Your help. In Jesus' name, Amen!

Maximizing Moments:
> Reread the Scriptures from today's reading and specifically ask yourself, "How can I be more intentional about living by these Scriptures?"

Maximizing Mantra:
> I cooperate with the law of the mind.

Day 32 – Maximizers Meditate

*"This book of the law shall not depart out of thy mouth;
but thou shalt meditate therein day and night, that thou mayest
observe to do according to all that is written therein:
for then thou shalt make thy way prosperous,
and then thou shalt have good success."*
Joshua 1:8 (KJV)

With what you have learned over the last couple of days, you are now ready to learn about biblical meditation. Now it is important for you to note that the term *biblical* is used intentionally as it relates to meditation. There are many forms of meditation, and you need to understand that the principles that you are learning are not adopted from some secular meditation course. Rather they are taken from the Bible. Even though there may be similarities, please know that what you are being exposed to now precedes all other forms of meditation.

Because you want to Maximize Your Life, you need to know that Maximizers meditate on God's Word! Yesterday you learned that experiences are the most powerful influencers on our belief system. What you personally experience will outweigh any other factor relative to what impacts your belief system. Biblical meditation, then, creates an intentional experience that will shape or reshape your belief and value system.

There are three types of experiences: natural, soulish, and spiritual. If you are going to maximize your biblical meditation, you must understand the different components of an experience. All experiences are comprised of words, images, and emotions. Whether it is natural, soulish, or spiritual, these three aspects will always be present. A natural experience is an event that actually occurs in your

Responsibility for Planning

life. (Remember, from yesterday, the chair example?) A soulish experience is an event that occurs in the arena of your mind like hypnosis, nightmares, dreams, and things that you imagine. Soulish experiences can be so real that you actually think they have occurred (like natural experiences). Have you ever had a dream that was so real that when you awoke, your heart rate was elevated and you were perspiring? Your mind and body did not distinguish this from a natural experience.

The third type of experience is a spiritual experience. A spiritual experience is very much like a soulish experience except that God initiates it through divine visions, or you can initiate it through meditation. Meditation provides us with spiritual experiences on the canvases of our imaginations that make potent impact on our value systems that either change or reinforce what we believe.

Since all experiences involve words, images, and emotions, a spiritual experience does as well. In the same way that the natural experience of the chair collapsing will change what you believe about that chair holding your weight, so will a soulish or spiritual experience affect what you will believe about any situation. Your subconscious locks in the information on that particular chair, and it will steer you away from it every time you enter the room.

Your conscience and subconscious work together in the decision-making process to keep you on a safe course in life. Neither one can distinguish between the various types of experiences. When a soulish or spiritual experience occurs repeatedly, the subconscious and conscience accept it as a real experience and make the necessary adjustments internally in the belief system and judgment process to keep you on the defined course.

Day 32 - Maximizers Meditate

As I said earlier, the Bible establishes these processes. There are many examples in the Bible where God uses a spiritual experience to inspire, encourage, and motivate people. The visions and dreams we often read or hear about in the Bible were God's method to motivate His people to action. Because God is a God of order, He will always work within the framework that He has established. So, in Ezekiel 37, God used a vision of dry bones to inspire the prophet to believe and preach that God would reunite His people as He had reunited the bones: *"I felt the power of the Lord on me, and he brought me out by the Spirit of the Lord and put me down in the middle of a valley. It was full of bones. He led me around among the bones, and I saw that there were many bones in the valley and that they were very dry. Then he asked me, 'Human, can these bones live?' I answered, 'Lord God, only you know.' He said to me, 'Prophesy to these bones and say to them, "Dry bones, hear the word of the Lord. This is what the Lord God says to the bones: I will cause breath to enter you so you will come to life""* (Ezekiel 37:1-5 NCV). Notice how God initiated this spiritual experience for Ezekiel. The impact it had on him was enormous, and he went and carried out exactly what God had told him to do.

There is another example in Genesis 13. God was developing Abram (Abraham) in faith for the bright future he had planned for him: *"After Lot had gone, the Lord said to Abram, 'Look as far as you can see in every direction—north and south, east and west. I am giving all this land, as far as you can see, to you and your descendants as a permanent possession. And I will give you so many descendants that, like the dust of the earth, they cannot be counted! Go and walk through the land in every direction, for I am giving it to you.' So Abram moved his camp to Hebron and settled near the oak grove belonging to Mamre. There he built another altar to the Lord"* (Genesis 13:14-18 NLT) .

Responsibility for Planning

As a result of this vision, Abram was inspired to believe what God had promised.

Another example of a spiritual experience that can change deep seated beliefs is in the New Testament. Peter was trained to be prejudiced against those outside of his old faith tradition. His prejudice was so extreme that he did not think Gentiles were worthy of the Gospel because they were not Jews. God gave Peter a vision to change his thinking: *"And he was hungry. But while a meal was being prepared, he fell into a trance. He saw the sky open, and something like a large sheet was let down by its four corners. In the sheet were all sorts of animals, reptiles, and birds. Then a voice said to him, 'Get up, Peter; kill and eat them.' 'No, Lord,' Peter declared. 'I have never eaten anything that our Jewish laws have declared impure and unclean.' But the voice spoke again: 'Do not call something unclean if God has made it clean.' The same vision was repeated three times. Then the sheet was suddenly pulled up to heaven. Peter was very perplexed. What could the vision mean? Just then the men sent by Cornelius found Simon's house. Standing outside the gate, . . . Then Peter replied, 'I see very clearly that God shows no favoritism. In every nation he accepts those who fear him and do what is right. This is the message of Good News for the people of Israel—that there is peace with God through Jesus Christ, who is Lord of all'"* (Acts 10:10-17; 34-36 NLT).

In a similar fashion, biblical meditation is a God-given method designed so that you can take the truth of God's Word and envision it having come to pass in your situation. When you do this repeatedly, it has tremendous effects on your belief system, your faith and ultimately, your life.

Day 32 - Maximizers Meditate

By definition, *meditation* means to mutter, muse over; to practice beforehand; to put to work; and to envision. You are actualizing in the realm of the spirit. This process is very simple and it starts with the Word of God and ends with praise to God. Tomorrow you will learn the mechanics of biblical meditation.

Maximized Prayer:
Father, I invite You to give me a spiritual experience that will help heal and refocus my life. I accept biblical meditation as Your method to reshape my beliefs and values so that I can complete my Maximized Life Journey. In Jesus' name, Amen.

Maximizing Moments:
Recall a natural experience that you had and how it changed your beliefs or values about a place, situation, or even person.

Do the same for a soulish experience.

If you have ever had a spiritual experience that changed your belief or values system, record it here.

Maximizing Mantra:
I maximize my life through biblical meditation.

Responsibility for Planning

NOTES

Day 33 – Mechanics of Meditation

*"This book of the law shall not depart out of thy mouth;
but thou shalt meditate therein day and night, that thou mayest
observe to do according to all that is written therein:
for then thou shalt make thy way prosperous,
and then thou shalt have good success."*
Joshua 1:8 (KJV)

Meditation is very much a biblical concept and necessary for Believers to move beyond the norm. As you learned yesterday, *meditation* means to mutter, muse over; to practice beforehand; to put to work; and to envision. There are three components of biblical meditation: verbalization, visualization, and internalization. These three elements encompass and address the basic components of an experience. You will recall, an experience is composed of words, emotions, and images.

Verbalization is the fundamental component of meditation. Whatever we desire when we meditate must be rooted in the Word of God—God's revealed will for His children. As you begin to speak God's words, several things happen. First, words create images. So when you speak what God's Word says about your circumstances and situation, you are able to produce a mental picture of what the will of God is for you.

Second, speaking the Word of God releases faith into the situation and triggers divine assistance:

"Jesus answered, 'Have faith in God. I tell you the truth, you can say to this mountain, 'Go, fall into the sea.' And if you have no doubts in your mind and believe that what you say will happen, God will do it for you. So I tell you to believe that you have received the things you ask for in prayer, and God will give them to you. When you are praying, if

you are angry with someone, forgive him so that your Father in heaven will also forgive your sins." (Mark 11:22-25 NCV)

"An evil man is ensnared by the transgression of his lips, but the righteous escapes from trouble." (Proverbs 12:13 ESV)

"The tongue can bring death or life; those who love to talk will reap the consequences." (Proverbs 18:21 NLT)

These verses clearly illustrate the importance of the words, which you speak.

Meditation starts with a biblical foundation. This is why pithy, feel-good statements are not biblical meditation. (This is the secular version of meditation, which is a perversion of God's system.) You were designed by God to respond to His Word. When you speak God's Word, a creative force is released to change your life (every situation and every problem).

The second component of biblical mediation is visualization. This term suggests being able to see or envision the object of meditation. All visualization must have a reference point. The ability to see what has not yet come to pass is possible and easier if there is a known model of what you desire.

The passages you read yesterday are poignant examples of the importance of visualization. God needed Abram (Abraham) and Ezekiel to see what the end result would be. They had no reference point of their own, so God had to give them an identifiable picture to which they could always refer. For some of the items that you are meditating, I recommend that you secure pictures of them. Or go to a place that represents a close representation of what you are expecting. There are so many Scriptures in the Bible where God uses what persons see to elevate their capacity to believe. The same is true for you (Genesis 15:1-6).

The third component of meditation is internalization. This component encompasses the appropriate corresponding action and emotion/affection, which anchors the meditation experience. The Bible instructs Believers to always be in control of their emotions. Knowing how to manage your emotions during meditation is essential to your success in this spiritual experience. You will be pleasantly surprised by how meaningful your meditation time becomes when you can control your emotions and allow the picture that you paint, based on the Word of God, to ignite a passion within you to see what you have visualized become a reality.

You have dreams of a better quality of life—a Maximized Life; that is why you are on this journey! God can fulfill those dreams if you will spend the time in meditation. If you paint a picture of your future on the canvas of your imagination, then you will draw closer and closer to seeing it. Meditation awakens in you everything that God has purposed for your life. When you spend time daily in meditation, you raise what you require for your life; and your subconscious will start to move you towards those things.

There must be a clear goal as you meditate. Internalization is part of the process to help galvanize the vision of your end result of your desire. Internalization is a dynamic process of acting out the desire at the level of your faith. It involves using vision enhancers, or props, to help clarify your vision. Then your subconscious process is triggered by this internalization. Tomorrow we will examine the importance of internally designing what is valued and how it stimulates your internal functions to move you in that direction.

Responsibility for Planning

Where there is clarity of vision, there is immediate acceleration toward the known goal. Have you ever been heading towards a known destination, a friend's home, work, or a different city? If, while you were traveling, fog descended and obscured your view, you would immediately decelerate to take into account the impeded vision. You would slow down and navigate cautiously and slowly to compensate for the obstructed vision caused by the fog. As soon as the fog would lift, your pace would accelerate. The same is true when you meditate. Once you have a clear goal, everything within you will move towards that known goal!

Now you can see the power of what God told Joshua: *"Study this Book of Instruction continually. Meditate on it day and night so you will be sure to obey everything written in it. Only then will you prosper and succeed in all you do"* (Joshua 1:8 NLT). Your success is tied to the time you spend in meditation based on the promises of God. Verbalize God's promises. Visualize your future and internalize your passions and affections towards that vision. These are the fundamental mechanics of meditation.

Maximized Prayer:

Father, I accept what You told Joshua as a word for my life! I will keep Your Word in my mouth, before my eyes, and in my mind through meditation. I expect results. In Jesus' name, Amen!

Maximizing Moments:

Now that you know how important visualization is, begin to gather pictures of things that approximate what your Maximized Life will look like. It may be a relationship, health, financial stability, etc. Find a picture! Or you can go to a place to jump start your vision process. You may look at model homes to get a sense of the new home you want to own. You can determine how many pictures you need.

Maximizing Mantra:

I have clarity of vision and accelerate towards my known goal!

Responsibility for Planning

NOTES

Day 34 – Garbage in, Garbage Out

"I praise you, for I am fearfully and wonderfully made. Wonderful are your works; my soul knows it very well."
Psalms 139:14 (ESV)

☞ What you believe will govern your life! These beliefs are deep-seated, as you have already learned. Once these have been programmed into your subconscious mind, there must be an intentional process to uproot contrary beliefs and establish proper beliefs. We now turn our attention to the subconscious mind.

Your subconscious mind is so powerful! Have you ever noticed that once you have repeatedly completed a task, to continue to perform it requires less and less of your conscious attention to do it? That is because your subconscious is gaining information every time you perform a task. It is learning. The mental intensity that it takes to perform familiar tasks decreases. Thus, your mind can multitask much more easily. Without the help of the subconscious mind, it would be difficult to do multiple tasks simultaneously like drive an automobile, look for an address, carry on a meaningful conversation, and eat a hamburger (this is not recommended!). Your subconscious serves as an autopilot that remembers actions.

This autopilot is vital to the stability of our personalities. Because the subconscious is always learning, it establishes truths that shape our self-images and cause us to have consistent behavioral characteristics. Without this assistance, it would be difficult to establish any form of consistency without intense, conscious effort. God leverages this to ensure the development and maintenance of godly character and faithfulness. This is why God can require faithfulness from you because He knows He built into you the capacity to remain consistent and loyal.

Responsibility for Planning

Without your subconscious, you would have to consciously rethink every moral decision that has already been taken every time you face a new decision. This would be very tedious and burdensome. However, if your subconscious is improperly formed, it will guide you away from the dreams and goals that you desire. Your subconscious is amoral; that is, it is neither good nor bad. Its function is to carry out its task of accessing your belief system standard and acting in agreement with it.

As you learned earlier, most of your beliefs and values are diametrically opposed to God's purpose and plan for your life. In fact, as you have moved through this journey, your subconscious has challenged some of this information and tried to discredit it. So most people need to alter the operation of the subconscious so that it will not intentionally work against their attainment of the Maximized Life. (This might be where you are also.)

If somewhere along life's way, you accepted something that was false as truth (because you really thought it was truth at that time), you misinformed your belief system. Your subconscious mind locked in on information that is false but thinks it's true. As a result, your subconscious—autopilot—has been operating and directing your life in agreement with something that is not true.

Here are some examples: You grew up in a home where you were told that all men are dogs. At every point, you saw your mom mistreated by men. Now you are a grown adult and find it difficult to have a stable, loving relationship with a man. It appears that every man you meet turns out to be a dog. You are wondering why it is that this keeps happening. It is because you have been programmed to believe a certain thing about men. And given the choice of two men—a good, honorable, loving, godly man or a dog, you always

Day 34 - Garbage In, Garbage Out

end up with the dog! Your autopilot goes searching for what it knows as truth. When you meet an authentically kind man, you reject him because his actions and persona do not line up with what you believe is the truth. In this way, your subconscious continues to lead you in the wrong direction but does not know it.

The same works with finances. It always seems like your financial breakthrough is always right outside your grasp. You grew up in a home that preached the scarceness of resources and how you must struggle for every penny. You were taught that life was supposed to be hard and then you die. Sure enough, as a grown man, you seem to never make ends meet. A lot of money passes through your hands, but you never get those financial ends to meet. Deals come up that others have prospered from and, when you try them, you lose money. You have questioned how it is that you always seem to come up short. You never associate the fact that your belief system is established in financial struggle; that is the truth that you were introduced to first. It is your truth until you dislodge it.

We can go on and on about examples of how your subconscious works against your goals because of improper programming. And the subconscious is so strong that it will attempt to block new, contrary information—even if that information is really the truth!

The language of the conscious and subconscious mind is three-dimensional: words, images, and emotions. These give birth to thoughts. Thoughts become images. Images elicit feelings and non-auditory communications on the screen of your imagination. The canvas of your imagination is like a motion picture big screen; on it, you see vivid pictures, sense feelings, and receive nonverbal messages.

Only when the subconscious mind is properly communicated with will the subconscious mind release an old, false truth and

Responsibility for Planning

assimilate the new truth into the conscience as new, reliable information. You will build your belief system based upon what you think about, experience, and meditate on. Even though you experience an event once, because you continue to think about it, you are creating a motion picture in your mind of that event. Unbeknownst to you, you are programming your subconscious concerning that event. Over a period of time, those vivid imaginations will enter your belief system and dislodge old information (Psalm 1:1-3).

In the computer field, there is an acronym: GIGO. It means "garbage in, garbage out"! When garbage has been lodged into your subconscious, it will lead you to more garbage and produce garbage in your life. However, if you put Truth in (with a capital T), then truth will come out. That truth is your Maximized Life!

Day 34 - Garbage In, Garbage Out

Maximized Prayer:

Father, I am like the blind man whom Jesus healed. I can honestly declare, "I once was blind but now I see." I see that I have some faulty information inside of me, and I take authority over it and begin the process of dislodging bad information through my meditation. In Jesus' name, Amen.

Maximizing Moments:

Time to be honest (brutally honest): If you look at your life, are there destructive patterns that repeat? (More often than not, these are caused by subconscious programming.) List them all. You cannot complete the Maximized Life Journey with garbage on the inside.

After you have listed the negative behaviors, here are your next steps:

- See yourself doing the right thing in those situations.
- Praise God for what you see on the canvas of your imagination. (This will communicate with your subconscious mind to release the old information and receive the new information.)

Maximizing Mantra:

My mind lines up with the Word of God!

NOTES

Day 35 – Take Out the Trash

"When the Spirit of truth comes, he will guide you into all truth. He will not speak on his own but will tell you what he has heard. He will tell you about the future."
John 16:13 (NLT)

Lest you think that this Journey is espousing some new psychology, you should know that because God oversees this process, He has given a vital Assistant (Helper) to guide us through this change process. He is the Holy Spirit.

The Bible speaks of the Holy Spirit's role in the life of the Believer to help you live the God-kind of life. And the existence of your brain, heart, or other organs does not diminish or neutralize the vital role that the Holy Spirit is designed to play in your spiritual growth.

The Holy Spirit works with the mental complex that you have learned about. So many people have been waiting for God to take certain behaviors away from them. They pray and believe that God is just going to take the urge away. However, this would violate the carefully orchestrated design of the mental complex. (There are instances where a person, as an act of the will, walks away from a destructive behavior immediately upon learning of its destructive affects; however, for most people, there is a process that must be followed.)

You will recall that the subconscious does not function solely independently of the conscious mind. It simply serves the conscious mind in the long-term operation of the belief system. This belief system is referred to as the conscience in the Scripture.

The conscious mind of the Believer depends on the Holy Spirit to communicate with it (to bear witness or affirm) to give guidance

Responsibility for Planning

and direction for living. More importantly, the conscious mind of the Believer depends on the Holy Spirit to help it determine what is true and what is not. Our Scripture reading today emphasizes the Holy Spirit's role in leading you into truth.

The Holy Spirit does this by communicating with your human spirit, who in turn gives relevant information to your conscious mind. You have called it an inspired thought, an idea. Many times you have said that something told you to do something. What you really heard was the voice of your human spirit. The following Scriptures provide biblical insight on the aforementioned interaction between the Holy Spirit, the human spirit, and the mind:

"And the Spirit himself joins with our spirits to say we are God's children." (Romans 8:16 NCV)

"God's Spirit has shown you everything. His Spirit finds out everything, even what is deep in the mind of God." (1 Corinthians 2:10 CEV)

Once the conscious mind receives information it deems to be reliable (in this case, spiritual truth) and validates it as truth, it allows the "right of passage" of that truth into the conscience to be accessed by the subconscious mind to automatically direct the Believer in line with the wishes of the Holy Spirit. You do not need to fear the subconscious mind. It only serves you based on what it has been instructed to do.

You are truly a marvelous creation!

You can alter your internal belief system, take out the trash, using this system. When God's Spirit (the Holy Spirit) is guiding your human spirit and mind, then you can accomplish anything! And remove any negative programming that has hindered your

Day 35 - Take Out the Trash

progress. When you meditate on the Word of God and visualize your maximized state, you begin to reprogram your inner system to accelerate towards your divine purpose.

Have you ever attended a significant event that left a powerful impression on you? The combination of words, images, and emotions gives you leverage to intentionally change the subconscious. Advertisers understand this! You can do for yourself what they do for the products they sell. Emotional information that is presented to you on a continuous basis will ultimately gain your mental consent (right of passage) and become a part of your belief system.

How do you break the destructive cycle of your subconscious? A conscious interrupt! Whenever the communications link between the subconscious mind and the conscience is interrupted by a conscious act, the subconscious operation process temporarily stops and awaits a conscious direction before proceeding. Your subconscious interprets this sudden interruption of its normal operation as something being out of order that must be corrected by the conscious mind. After a series of consecutive interruptions, the subconscious mind tends to accept and assimilate the new, conscious response as the appropriate one and releases the old, automatic response.

How you automatically respond to certain situations can be changed by a conscious interrupt. For example, if something tragic happened to you years ago as you were driving around a sharp curve, this experience caused damaging negative information about driving around sharp curves to be stored in your belief system (conscience). Every time you approach a sharp curve in the road, your subconscious accesses the information and sends out distress signals

Responsibility for Planning

all through your body. In essence, the subconscious sends this message: "We are in danger; sharp curves cause tragic accidents." So the message is sent throughout your body for the heart to beat faster; for you to take short, panting breaths; for palms to begin to sweat; for breathing to become difficult; and for muscles to tense up. Instantly, you are gripped with fear.

To overcome this erroneous response of the subconscious, you must consciously interrupt this subconscious action. For instance, if you will stop and take a deep breath, the whole automatic process stops and awaits further instructions. After you do this on each occasion and successfully navigate the curve, the entire fear cycle is replaced by a confidence cycle.

With the simple knowledge gained today, you can interrupt any subconscious response and take control of it. This will allow you to overcome any phobia, restrictive behavior, or destructive pattern. As you intentionally manage this interrupt process, you will take out all the trash in your subconscious.

Maximized Prayer:
Today's prayer is replaced with time for meditation. See yourself overcoming these situations. Also, starting today, commit at least 15 minutes per day for meditation purposes. Begin to practice what you are learning.

Maximizing Moments:
Are you conditioned to act a certain way that you wish you could stop? What is it? Decide right now what conscious interrupt you will employ when your subconscious begins to act. Identify a Scripture to assist in this process.

Maximizing Mantra:
I submit to the Holy Spirit's guidance to lead me.

Responsibility for Planning

NOTES

DAY 36 – 12 STEPS TO SUCCESS

*"On the glorious splendor of your majesty,
and on your wondrous works, I will meditate."*
Psalm 145:5 (ESV)

Today is a significant day in your journey because you have the opportunity to apply the principles of biblical meditation, which will assist you in rapidly making the midcourse correction you desire. These steps will work if you diligently implement them to set clear-cut vision goals.

Step 1: Decide the end result in a particular area of life. (This must be scripturally based.) Write this down in very forceful terms. Here is an example: "I will be a loving, compassionate, sensitive parent who will spend 30 minutes each day talking to my child, giving my child my undivided attention." A goal is a measurable objective and not an abstract or wishful thought! If the progressive results cannot be measured, it is not a goal!

Step 2: Envision yourself on the internal screen of your imagination as though your goal has been accomplished. See yourself as the person doing what you stated you would do in Step 1. In this case, you see yourself talking and enjoying time with your child.

Step 3: Estimate how long it should realistically take you to become the person you envision. This step adds some accountability to your targeted desire.

Step 4: List the people who will assist you in obtaining this goal (these are resources that you already have). This step may call for resource materials such as books, magazines, or support groups that help develop discipline in certain areas.

Responsibility for Planning

Step 5: Think on how you are going to use the resources and how you have possibly used them in the past. Schedule the use of these resources or support groups in the framework of your week.

Step 6: Envision the people whose lives you will affect the most, who will benefit from the person you will be after achieving these goals. This step anchors your desire and effort with a positive purpose; it provides the "important why" that serves as motivation.

Step 7: Think of someone you know who has achieved this goal and write down his/her name. Now you have a natural example, which is most important for natural development towards success.

Step 8: Take time now to draft a step-by-step plan of action on the best way to go about achieving this goal. Remember, it's only a draft. You'll probably change it later. The more you do this, the more clearly you will see how to make it happen. This is the unique way that God works in us to help us develop workable plans of action.

Step 9: Now think about the last time you accomplished something worthwhile. Begin to thank God for His goodness and blessings in your life. For best results, close your eyes and think about the peace and satisfaction and confidence you have in God based on what He has done for you in the past and what you envision Him doing in your future. David, the shepherd boy, prepared himself to win over Goliath by using this step; he rehearsed his past successes: *"But David persisted. 'I have been taking care of my father's sheep and goats,' he said. 'When a lion or a bear comes to steal a lamb from the flock, I go after it with a club and rescue the lamb from its mouth. If the animal turns on me, I catch it by the jaw and club it to death. I have done this to both lions and bears, and I'll do it to this pagan Philistine, too, for he has defied the armies of the living God'"* (1

Samuel 17:34-36 NLT)! This step is far more important than you think. You are now adding a positive emotional component to the pursuit of this desire, the last component of what defines an experience: words, images, and emotions.

Step 10: Now reinforce Step 9 by seeing yourself having completed the goal. Begin to praise God that by faith it is done. See on the canvas of your imagination the joy you have brought to others because of this effort and thank God that He has made it possible. This step is what the Bible calls the sacrifice of praise that, according to Scripture, triggers divine help to accomplish your goal.

Step 11: Repeat as often as you possibly can Steps 9 and 10. This repetition will enrich you. This repetitious meditation will trigger the faculties of the mental complex to help you chart the course and perform according to plan until your goal is achieved. In both passages, Joshua 1:8 and Psalm 1:3, the Bible uses the phrase "meditate day and night," which suggests continuous repetition.

Step 12: After performing Step 11 continuously, you will begin to receive more insight into a workable plan of action. Return to Step 8 and refine your plan based on this newly acquired information and follow Steps 9 through 11 until your goal is reached.

These steps will lead you to the victory that you seek. As you learn more life-changing principles for the rest of this journey, you will gain more spiritual tools.

Responsibility for Planning

Maximizing Moments:
(Today, there is no Maximized Prayer or Maximizing Mantra.) Take the rest of your time to create a mediation plan that will guide you to your Maximized Life. (Use the Maximized Life Journey Passport to capture this plan.)

Day 37 – Take the DARE

"Brothers and sisters, I know that I have not yet reached that goal, but there is one thing I always do. Forgetting the past and straining toward what is ahead."
Philippians 3:13 (NCV)

For the life you seek, the Maximized Life, you will need to establish a level of discontentment (unbearable pain) with where you are in life today and link massive amounts of pleasure to your desired behavior. You will then direct your God-given faculties to accelerate the change process. Once your personal awareness function and your internal guidance function of the subconscious are activated through meditation by the new image that you have, you will be well on your way.

You need to take the DARE! DARE to rise above where you are and attain the Maximized Life that God has ordained for you from the foundations of the earth! The DARE is a proven method that will assist you in reaching and maintaining your most resourceful state. The DARE Method is defined as deciding, associating, recollecting, and envisioning.

Decide: You must decide what you need to change and what you want to be like afterwards. Be sure to be directed by the Word of God to verify that the desired change is in fact in agreement with the expressed will of God. Write this down with as much graphic detail as possible.

Associate: You must associate pain to the old behavior and pleasure to the results of making the change. This is the most important step to initiate the change. There are two aspects to this step: List the worst possible things that will be the end results of not changing, and list the results and superior sense of fulfillment you will have and enjoy as a result of making the change.

Responsibility for Planning

Recollect: You must recall the experiences that have hindered your decision to follow through on the previous decision to change. Normally, the pain and emotions associated with the past have so anchored the belief that change seems to be impossible. Until this self-defeated belief is properly processed and dealt with, change will not take place. To rid yourself of this blockage, you must confess the blood of Jesus over the old experience to disassociate (unlock) the emotions from the old experience.

Never forget this truth: You were designed to move from pain towards pleasure. The more pleasurable the vision of your new state becomes, the more motivated your mind will be to move in that direction. This process may sound strange, but it is a biblical principle. Paul modeled this principle. He intentionally forgot those things that came before and pursued the goal, which lay ahead of him. In fact, Paul called his prior life rubbish!

There is a spiritual promise that can accomplish the elimination of the pain often associated with events. The Bible is filled with promises of God for the Believer to improve the quality of their lives: *"We use God's mighty weapons, not worldly weapons, to knock down the strongholds of human reasoning and to destroy false arguments"* (2 Corinthians 10:4 NLT).

You often hear Christians talking about the blood of Jesus. There is a divine, spiritual power released to help cleanse our conscience, to eradicate the pain of past events and situations when a Believer affirms the promise of the blood of Jesus. The Bible does not use the word *affirm*; it uses the word *confession* (Romans 10:10). This word means to say in agreement with God. So, then, to confess the Word of God is to say with your mouth, "Father, thank You for the power of Your blood which now cleanses the pain of every

Day 37 – Take the DARE

negative emotion from my past. In Jesus' name, Amen." Now this may sound strange; but it is not strange. It is spiritual and scriptural: *"The blood of goats and bulls and the ashes of a cow are sprinkled on the people who are unclean, and this makes their bodies clean again. How much more is done by the blood of Christ. He offered himself through the eternal Spirit as a perfect sacrifice to God. His blood will make our consciences pure from useless acts so we may serve the living God"* (Hebrews 9:13-14 NCV).

This passage states that, just as in the Old Testament when the blood of a sacrifice was used to provide spiritual cleansing for the nation, so now does the blood of Jesus provide spiritual cleansing for our minds. We apply the spiritual promises through the confession of our mouths and the belief in our hearts in an unfailing God.

So then, although it is not possible to erase the memory of an event from our minds, it is possible to erase and eradicate completely the emotional pain of the negative situations and events from your past. This will accomplish the elimination of the negative influences of past events on your future decision making, which impacts the quality of life.

Forgetting is one of the most difficult things to do because it's almost impossible to erase or discard something from your memory. Forgetting is not difficult when you think in terms of detachment of emotions associated with an event, which sometimes reoccurs over a period of time. This exercise accomplishes the detachment of emotions associated with past events.

Envision: You must see yourself as totally the "new you" like your mentor or model. See yourself in the same dynamic posture and behavior pattern that your models use when they look and act confident. This imagery will change your internal self-image.

Responsibility for Planning

Remember, the more you meditate on this, the more the mind experiences this and sets your internal subconscious faculties in motion to assist you in bringing it to pass. Always end the spiritual experience of meditation with thanking and praising God for the Maximized person that you are becoming and the Maximized Life that you will be living.

DARE to close the door on the past and walk into a bright future!

<u>**Maximized Prayer:**</u>
>Father, I acknowledge the power of the blood of Jesus. Your Word promises that it cleanses me from every dead work. I receive Your power to release me from the pain of my past and move me forward towards my Maximized Life. I rejoice now in Jesus' name, Amen.

<u>**Maximizing Moments:**</u>
>Today list all those past negative experiences that you need to forget about. Use the DARE method to plan a way forward.

<u>**Maximizing Mantra:**</u>
>My pain is erased by the blood of Jesus.

DAY 38 – LIVE GENEROUSLY

*"The generous will prosper;
those who refresh others will themselves be refreshed."*
Proverbs 11:25 (NLT)

Earlier on your Maximized Life Journey, you learned about prosperity and the strategies to produce abundance in your life. For the next several days, you will be exposed to revolutionary information on giving and living a generous life! Because you want to Maximize Your Life, you will need to grasp these principles and put them into practice to see biblical prosperity manifest! All it takes is obedience to God's Word in the area of giving and you will find another level of living.

This level of living will recession-proof your life because what you learn over the next couple of days will start a flow of blessings into your life that will never stop! Let's look at what the Bible says about giving:

"Be generous: Invest in acts of charity. Charity yields high returns. Don't hoard your goods; spread them around. Be a blessing to others. This could be your last night." (Ecclesiastes 11:1 MSG)

"In the morning sow your seed, and in the evening withhold not your hands, for you know not which shall prosper, whether this or that, or whether both alike will be good." (Ecclesiastes 11:6 AMP)

"They weep as they go to plant their seed, but they sing as they return with the harvest." (Psalm 126:6 NLT)

"If a person asks you for something, give it to him. Don't refuse to give to someone who wants to borrow from you." (Matthew 5:42 NCV)

"Looking at the man, Jesus felt genuine love for him. 'There is still one thing you haven't done,' he told him. 'Go and sell all your possessions and give the money to the poor, and you will have treasure in heaven. Then come, follow me.'" (Matthew 19:21 NLT)

"Each of you must make up your own mind about how much to give. But don't feel sorry that you must give and don't feel that you are forced to give. God loves people who love to give." (2 Corinthians 9:7 CEV)

"Give freely and become more wealthy; be stingy and lose everything." (Proverbs 11:24 NLT)

There are so many other Scriptures to affirm the importance of giving. God endorses neither greed nor stinginess. However, He does expect generosity from His children! In fact, He uses it as a measure by which to bless you: *"Give, and you will receive. You will be given much. Pressed down, shaken together, and running over, it will spill into your lap. The way you give to others is the way God will give to you"* (Luke 6:38 NCV).

Your giving entitles you to financial increase! An entitlement is an earned or bestowed position of favor, advantage, or privilege. You will increase in life to the degree that you are able to both recognize and respond to divine opportunities for increase. You may rightfully ask at this point, "What is a divine opportunity for increase?" The answer is very simple: any opportunity to give!

God's path to financial increase comes from giving! There is no other way! Many people are fascinated by lotteries, casinos, games of chance, and "get rich quick" schemes as roadways to the financial prosperity that they seek; and more than a few of them have ended up on the side of the road in a financial ditch. Others attempt to

Day 38 - Live Generously

work multiple jobs while ignoring their families, leisure activities, and their health. In the end, though they may have amassed considerable financial resources, they cannot enjoy them because they have spent their strength trying to prosper without God. Giving is 100% certain to generate returns in your life—without stress, strain, or struggle!

Every opportunity to give is an opportunity to be blessed! Think of it this way: Consider all that God has done for you in life. Remember all the times He has delivered you out of situations that seemed impossible. Reflect upon His great love for you demonstrated on Calvary's cross. Based on all this, you will give to Him because you love Him! In fact, everything that you have comes from the benevolent hand of God! You will recall when David and Israel gave to build the Temple; they offered what is probably the biggest one-day offering in history! At the end of all the giving, David humbly acknowledged the source of all his blessings: *"But me—who am I, and who are these my people, that we should presume to be giving something to you? Everything comes from you; all we're doing is giving back what we've been given from your generous hand"* (1 Chronicles 29:14 MSG).

So, even though you give to God out of love, it is He who established giving as the way to bless your life! The level of living that God wants you to have is the blessed life—nothing less: *"The blessing of the Lord makes a person rich, and he adds no sorrow with it"* (Proverbs 10:22 NLT). God wants to make you rich—abundantly supplied—if you will submit to His plan. You should give to God based on principle, not emotion. This derails so many Believers because they allow their feelings to govern their giving. But when you understand the importance of giving, you will do it based on

Revolutionary Planting

principle! As a Maximizer, that's your goal: to be abundantly supplied so that you can use your money *"to do good"* and to *"be rich in good works and generous to those in need, always being ready to share with others"* (1 Timothy 6:18 NLT). You were created by God to do good works. Do you see how your abundance will directly fulfill the purpose for your life?

From the foundations of the world, you were designed to benefit someone other than yourself: *"For we are His workmanship, created in Christ Jesus for good works, which God prepared beforehand that we should walk in them"* (Ephesians 2:10 NKJ). When you can bless others, you are fulfilling the reason you were put on the earth. No longer do you need to wonder about your purpose; just do good works! And God is ready to give you the resources if you commit to live generously!

Let's end today looking at what God does in response to your giving: *"And God will generously provide all you need. Then you will always have everything you need and plenty left over to share with others. As the Scriptures say, 'They share freely and give generously to the poor. Their good deeds will be remembered forever.' For God is the one who provides seed for the farmer and then bread to eat. In the same way, he will provide and increase your resources and then produce a great harvest of generosity in you. Yes, you will be enriched in every way so that you can always be generous. And when we take your gifts to those who need them, they will thank God"* (2 Corinthians 9:8-11 NLT).

Maximized Prayer:
Father, You set the example for giving. I set my heart to operate like You. I accept my purpose to bless others. I will obey You in my giving so that I can walk in abundance. In Jesus' name, Amen.

Maximizing Moments:
Would you characterize yourself as generous?

What type of tipper are you?

How often do you randomly bless others?

Maximizing Mantra:
I am blessed to be a blessing!

NOTES

DAY 39 – OPEN THE WINDOWS

*"Bring your full tithe to the Temple treasury
so there will be ample provisions in my Temple."*
Malachi 3:10 (NLT)

Today you will be learning about the foundational element of giving: the tithe. All giving to the Kingdom of God starts with tithing. While tithing is not a new biblical concept, it is often misunderstood or rejected by people who say it does not apply today. However, tithing is in the Bible and active for the New Testament Believer. Since giving entitles you to financial increase, you must start by obeying God in paying your tithes.

Tithing is giving ten (10) percent of your income (increase) to God's house (the place where you receive spiritual nourishment). Tithing is seen in the Old and New Testaments. Abram (Abraham) first demonstrated tithing. Abram's nephew Lot, while a resident in Sodom, had been kidnapped and taken into captivity as a prisoner of war. Abram took 318 of the servants and went to war against the foreign king. Having launched a surprise attack, they overtook the enemy and recovered everything that had been taken, including Lot and everything he owned.

The King of Sodom met Abram on his way home (Genesis 14:14-17). Before Abram could interact with the King of Sodom, Melchizedek, King of Salem and Priest of God, brought Abram a meal of bread and wine (symbolizing communion). Melchizedek pronounced a blessing upon Abram: *"Then Abram gave Melchizedek a tenth of everything he had brought back from the battle"* (Genesis 14:20 NCV). Without a law or mandate, Abram, out of the genuineness of his heart, knew to offer the priest a tenth of the spoils from war. Clearly, Abram had a conviction about his giving and its association with receiving because as soon as he honored God with the tithe, the

King of Sodom tried to bestow financial blessings on Abram. But Abram refused: *"Abram answered: The LORD God Most High made the heavens and the earth. And I have promised him that I won't keep anything of yours, not even a sandal strap or a piece of thread. Then you can never say that you are the one who made me rich"* (Genesis 14:22-23 CEV).

Here is Abram, with no Bible at all, honoring God with the tithe! He understood that honoring God with the tithe would bring him blessings. The principle of tithing was also practiced by Jacob in Genesis 28:22.

As time went on, Israel needed to be reminded of this fundamental spiritual truth about the tithe. So, 430 years later, the tithe was included in the law: *"And all the tithe of the land, whether of the seed of the land or of the fruit of the tree, is the Lord's; it is holy to the Lord"* (Leviticus 27:30 AMP). God included tithing in the law because He wanted to keep the justifiable right to bless Israel. Without the tithe, He could not because tithing is a law in and of itself. And it works for anyone who works it. Once tithing was codified in the law, Israel faithfully did it. And those who are faithful Jews have continued it.

The New Testament Church, which was founded by faithful Jews, assumed (in principle) the law of the tithe. Jesus, Himself, affirmed that the tithe did not pass away with the law: *"What sorrow awaits you teachers of religious law and you Pharisees. Hypocrites! For you are careful to tithe even the tiniest income from your herb gardens, but you ignore the more important aspects of the law—justice, mercy, and faith. You should tithe, yes, but do not neglect the more important things"* (Matthew 23:23 NLT). If the tithe were not applicable for today, this would have been the ideal time for Jesus to renounce it.

Day 39 - Open the Windows

But, because Jesus wants His people blessed, He could not revoke the law of the tithe! In fact, the New Testament even goes further to explain the significance of the tithe.

In the Book of Hebrews, the writer revisits the exchange between Abram (Abraham) and Melchizedek. He affirms the spiritual nature of their exchange: *"But Melchizedek, who was not a descendant of Levi, collected a tenth from Abraham. And Melchizedek placed a blessing upon Abraham, the one who had already received the promises of God. And without question, the person who has the power to give a blessing is greater than the one who is blessed. The priests who collect tithes are men who die, so Melchizedek is greater than they are, because we are told that he lives on"* (Hebrews 7:6-8 ESV). There is always an exchange that takes place when the tithe is paid. While you pay your tithes here on earth, Jesus is in heaven receiving them and placing them on the heavenly altar.

Your tithe provides ample provisions for the work of God. As you pay your tithes, you ensure that the place from which you hear the Word of God (local church) is able to continue promoting the Gospel of Jesus Christ. When you arrived at your local church, there were ample provisions for you to receive the Word. And your giving continues that flow of ample provisions for others to come and receive the Word of God. When a church has more, it can do more. Each church needs sufficient resources to carry out its mission. You should rejoice as you pay your tithes that there is an abundance of resources for God's work to continue. You honor God with your tithe! You demonstrate to God that you acknowledge He has given you everything you have and you will be obedient in giving Him what belongs to Him. The tithe represents the minimum financial commitment the Believer has to God.

Revolutionary Planting

And when you pay your tithes to God in your local church, a spiritual exchange takes place. You give your natural and Heaven releases the supernatural blessing over your life: *"I will open the windows of heaven for you. I will pour out a blessing so great you won't have enough room to take it in! Try it! Put me to the test"* (Malachi 3:10 NLT). When the windows are open over your life, you will receive divine opportunities and insight. Most people miss the fact that the blessing from tithing is not money, that if they give God $100, He will give them $1000. God has promised more than money. He will pour out divine opportunities in abundance so that you will not be able to take advantage of them all. Further, God promises to protect the increase that He gives you (Malachi 3:11).

A divine opportunity is an arrangement of favorable situations, which seeks your participation and whose future return should far outweigh the present investment. You will increase to the degree that you recognize and respond to opportunities. Opportunity does not knock but stands silently by disguised as a problem and normally goes unnoticed because initially it looks like an unfair exchange. As a tither, you should expect opportunities and respond appropriately to them. As you do, you will increase financially.

Maximizers give the tithe and have justifiable expectations that God has opened the windows of Heaven over their lives. A Maximizer will never rob God. You should pray for blessings and release faith for the promises because you are a tither. You are prequalified for them. (Continue to follow the strategies that you learned on Days 22 and 23.)

Maximized Prayer:

Day 39 - Open the Windows

Father, I choose to participate in your plan to bless my life. I will pay my tithes consistently so that Your work can continue in the earth, and I stand in high expectation for divine opportunities and insight to manifest in my life. In Jesus' name, Amen.

Maximizing Moments:

Do you tithe? (If not, examine your heart. What is keeping you from obeying God?)

Reflect on your life. Are there opportunities that you passed up because they appeared like unfair exchanges? Were you given insight into a problem and you never acted on it?

Maximizing Mantra:

There is an open window over my life!

NOTES

DAY 40 – SEED FAITH GIVING

"Each of you should give as you have decided in your heart to give. You should not be sad when you give, and you should not give because you feel forced to give. God loves the person who gives happily."
2 Corinthians 9:7 (NCV)

Now that you have a revelation (understanding) of tithing, it's time to talk about offerings. "What? You mean God wants more of my money?" Well, let's clarify some things. First, the tithe belongs to God! It is not yours. Thus, having paid your tithe, you have only returned to God what belongs to Him. When you withhold it, God calls it stealing. The tithe is the minimum commitment of the Believer. It is minimum obedience. God told the Israelites that they were robbing Him in tithes *and offerings* (Malachi 3:8)! God expects His children to bring Him offerings!

If you want to live a supernatural life, you must pay your tithes and give offerings. A supernatural life is an extraordinary, exceptional lifestyle that the Believer lives as a result of following biblical principles. So what is Seed Faith Giving? It is an intentional investment based on a godly principle that can handle an existing need, a future need, or desire. Seed Faith Giving is the plan of God to take you to that place of supernatural abundance and favor: *"Knowing that whatever good anyone does, he will receive the same from the Lord, whether he is a slave or free"* (Ephesians 6:8 NKJ).

So when you make a commitment to make something happen for someone else, God gets involved. Whenever God gets involved, it's supernatural. When you target your giving intentionally and start to make things happen for others, God gets involved to make the same thing happen for you. When you live by this type of giving, you will walk in whole life prosperity—every area of your life will be blessed. When you give, you cannot see it as money going into a bank: *"For ever since the world was created, people have seen the earth and sky. Through everything God made, they can clearly see his invisible qualities—his eternal power and divine nature. So they have no excuse for not knowing God"* (Romans 1:20 NLT). God uses the natural things that you can see to explain—make understandable to you—His invisible ways. So, in order for you to understand what is happening when you give over and above your tithe, that is, giving offerings, you are sowing seed.

Now you see the results of sowing seed all around you. From the fruit you eat to the grass you walk on, it all came about because of seed sown in the soil. In like manner, you must see your giving of offerings as seed sown into soil; and it must produce a harvest. If you can understand the seed principle in nature, you will understand how your giving will work: *"Remember this—a farmer who plants only a few seeds will get a small crop. But the one who plants generously will get a generous crop. You must each decide in your heart how much to give. And don't give reluctantly or in response to pressure. For God loves a person who gives cheerfully"* (2 Corinthians 9:6-7 NLT). Your giving is like a farmer sowing seed. And, if you give (sow) sparingly, you will reap sparingly.

Here are some general understandings of sowing seed:

- A seed looks nothing like what it can become. But it is preprogrammed to produce. When the seed is planted, its programming is activated to produce a harvest.
- You will always reap in a greater measure than you sow.
- You will always reap later than when you sow. It will take some time, but it works! It must come to pass. All of heaven's integrity is depending on it.

Day 40 - Seed Faith Giving

- There cannot be a harvest without sowing. You determine in advance the size of your harvest based on what you sow.

Your giving supernaturally impacts more than the offering plate. It's not about just paying bills at the church. It sets into motion blessings—supernatural blessings—coming towards you: *"And God is able to make all grace abound toward you, that you, always having all sufficiency in all things, may have an abundance for every good work"* (2 Corinthians 9:8 NKJ).

Grace (favor) is the willingness of others to use their power, ability, and influence to help you! When you sow your seed, God puts you on someone's mind for them to help you. Something happens when you release money out of your hand. It leaves your hand, but it never leaves your life.

Look at one situation in Scripture where God gets involved based on offerings: *"Then the offering of Judah and Jerusalem will be pleasing to the LORD as in the days of old and as in former years. Then I will draw near to you for judgment. I will be a swift witness against the sorcerers, against the adulterers, against those who swear falsely, against those who oppress the hired worker in his wages, the widow and the fatherless, against those who thrust aside the sojourner, and do not fear me, says the LORD of hosts"* (Malachi 3:4-5 ESV). In this prophetic Scripture, God says He will get involved on the basis of His children's offerings.

You can sow a seed for God to get involved in negative situations against you! God will show up quickly on your behalf and judge the situation. Whether it is someone using manipulation against you, someone encroaching on your marriage, someone lying on you, someone withholding wages from you, or someone taking

Revolutionary Planting

advantage of you because you are in a vulnerable position, God will judge it in your favor! And your seed faith giving will make it work.

Now, up to this point, you have seen the seed explained. It becomes seed faith giving when you stand in faith for the preprogrammed harvest based on the seed you have sown. When you target your giving towards a biblical promise and you continue to confess that promise over what you have sown, it will produce in your life. Over the next couple of days, you will see specific examples of how seed faith giving works.

People who are not spiritually minded will challenge this type of giving. But not you! You understand that God wants to maximize every part of your life and that includes your money! Begin to live by your giving and you will experience a level of supernatural living that you never thought was possible (Proverbs 10:22; Deuteronomy 8:18; Mark 10:30).

Maximized Prayer:
Father, I am not afraid to give! I push past all resistance to seed faith giving. My offerings invite You to get involved in my situation! I rejoice in Your plan to bring me into a supernatural lifestyle. In Jesus' name, Amen.

Maximizing Moments:
What kind of giver are you? Do you intentionally and regularly give over and above your tithe? Do you target your giving towards certain promises?

What are reasons that have kept you from sowing seed regularly?

What situations are you facing that you need God to judge? Today set apart a seed for that need (make certain, when the next opportunity comes to give, you will sow the seed). Then stand in faith that it is done!

Maximizing Mantra:
What I make happen for others, God makes happen for me!

Notes

DAY 41 – HONORING GOD'S SERVANTS

"Let him who receives instruction in the Word [of God] share all good things with his teacher [contributing to his support]."
Galatians 6:6 (AMP)

Now that you understand the importance of sowing seed, it is imperative that you leverage this principle for maximum results in your life. One area where you should target your seed is into the life of God's servant—your pastor. Some resist this because they do not value the spiritual role that God's servant plays in their lives. The Bible is clear that those who lead churches and serve in ministry capacities are His servants. And they are His gift to you: *"And I will give you shepherds after my own heart, who will guide you with knowledge and understanding"* (Jeremiah 3:15 NLT).

When someone, or something, has been given to you, how you treat that gift will send a signal to the giver about your gratitude. Society has sown seeds of doubt about those who serve in pastoral roles and distorted the good work that they have done because of a few bad examples. However, you should not throw the baby out with the bath water. Honoring God's servants is very much biblical and Maximizers are not intimidated to go against the grain and obey God: *"Elders who do their work well should be respected and paid well, especially those who work hard at both preaching and teaching. For the Scripture says, 'You must not muzzle an ox to keep it from eating as it treads out the grain.' And in another place, 'Those who work deserve their pay'"* (1 Timothy 5:17-18 NLT).

Those who faithfully serve God and God's people are more than entitled to have those whom they teach give into their lives. Our reading for today supports this. God has no problem with His servants being blessed. And the people whose lives are positively

Revolutionary Planting

impacted by their ministry should show that gratitude to God by honoring His servants.

An often-quoted Scripture has not been given its full context and, as a result, Believers have missed the powerful principle behind it: *"And my God shall supply all your need according to His riches in glory by Christ Jesus"* (Philippians 4:19 NKJ). Many quote this and expect to see the manifestation of it in their lives. However, this verse was targeted at Believers who honored God's servant enough to provide for his financial support: *"But it was right and commendable and noble of you to contribute for my needs and to share my difficulties with me. And you Philippians yourselves well know that in the early days of the Gospel ministry, when I left Macedonia, no church (assembly) entered into partnership with me and opened up [a debit and credit] account in giving and receiving except you only. For even in Thessalonica you sent [me contributions] for my needs, not only once but a second time"* (Philippians 4:14-16 AMP).

Paul commended the Philippians for their generosity in supporting him financially. And, because they had obeyed God, Paul was assured that God would provide for all their need. In like manner, because you believe in seed faith giving, when you give to support God's servant, you can expect God to supply all your need! This is not just financial need but all your needs! Giving to support God's servants is a way that God uses to meet your need!

Paul was not manipulating them! He was very clear that there was a principle at work: *"I am not trying to get something from you, but I want you to receive the blessings that come from giving"* (Philippians 4:17 CEV). Look at that verse in another translation: *"Not that I seek or am eager for [your] gift, but I do seek and am eager for the fruit which increases to your credit [the harvest of blessing that is*

Day 41 - Honoring God's Servants

accumulating to your account]" (AMP). God will give you a first-class lifestyle as you support God's servant! It will be supernatural because God gets involved.

It was protocol in the Old Testament that, when a person approached God's servant, he brought a gift. When Saul's donkeys were lost and they could not find them, Saul and his servant sought for God's servant to help them: *"'Wait!' the servant answered. ' There's a man of God who lives in a town near here. He's amazing! Everything he says comes true. Let's talk to him. Maybe he can tell us where to look. Saul said, 'How can we talk to the prophet when I don't have anything to give him? We don't even have any bread left in our sacks. What can we give him?' 'I have a small piece of silver,' the servant answered. 'We can give him that, and then he will tell us where to look for the donkeys'"* (1 Samuel 9:6-8 CEV).

If you grasp this revelation (understanding) of honoring God's servant, you will accelerate your Maximized Life Journey. Honoring God's servant means to give fitting and due respect, recognition, and resources. You give fitting and due respect by remembering that servants of God are called by God and commissioned by God; thus, they are serving a vital spiritual role in your life. You should never become common with a servant of God to the point that you devalue the role that God has that person play in your life: *"Now these are the gifts Christ gave to the church: the apostles, the prophets, the evangelists, and the pastors and teachers. Their responsibility is to equip God's people to do his work and build up the church, the body of Christ"* (Ephesians 4:11-12 NLT).

Fitting and due recognition is given when you formally honor God's servant. Some churches dedicate a Sunday per year to allow the people an opportunity to recognize the work of God's servant. It

Revolutionary Planting

is right that God's servant who labors faithfully be recognized. So much is said negatively against preachers. Those who are doing what God has called them to do should be recognized and honored.

You give fitting and due resources by dedicating monetary gifts for God's servants. This may be a formal gift given during times of recognition. Or it may be as God moves on your heart to give at a specific time. Some churches even allow the members to give to God's servant through the Sunday offering envelope. Whatever the method, it is right to give fitting and due resources to God's servant.

Honor given to God's servant is matter of divine calling, compensation, and care. As you have seen, God calls His servants to perform the work that they do. He also has set the compensation for His servants: *"No soldier ever serves in the army and pays his own salary. No one ever plants a vineyard without eating some of the grapes. No person takes care of a flock without drinking some of the milk. I do not say this by human authority; God's law also says the same thing. It is written in the law of Moses: 'When an ox is working in the grain, do not cover its mouth to keep it from eating.' When God said this, was he thinking only about oxen? No. He was really talking about us. Yes, that Scripture was written for us, because it goes on to say: 'The one who plows and the one who works in the grain should hope to get some of the grain for their work.' Since we planted spiritual seed among you, is it too much if we should harvest material things"* (1 Corinthians 9:7-11 NCV)? And God has set the standard of care.

Having honored God's servant, you can have a justifiable expectation that manifested grace will be on your life. Paul told the Philippians, *"They were partakers of his grace"* (Philippians 1:7). Every victory that Paul won, every soul that was saved through Paul's ministry, every witness Paul gave of the Gospel, they were

Day 41 - Honoring God's Servants

participants in it. And Paul knew that they could win in every situation because they functioned in the same grace that was on his life. This is the expectation you should have as you give to support God's servants; take advantage of this!

You, as a Maximizer, will give to God's servant because it pleases God. The objections of others who do not understand will not detour you. And when you make a natural decision to do something in your life and with your life that glorifies God, you trigger the supernatural power and grace of God to bring it to pass. You will never regret your decision to honor God's servants.

Revolutionary Planting

Maximized Prayer:
Father, thank You for the gift that You gave to me in my pastor! I will give to Your servant due and fitting respect, recognition, and resources so that I will live a first-class lifestyle. In Jesus' name, Amen.

Maximizing Moments:
Write down all the blessings you have received from the ministry in which you are set.

Write down the messages that you have heard that have given you new understanding and strength to make it.

Do something today to honor the servant that God has placed in your life.

Maximizing Mantra:
My pastor is God's gift to me!

DAY 42 – VOW AND PAY

*"You will make your prayer to Him,
He will hear you, And you will pay your vows."*
Job 22:27 (NKJ)

God has given His Word to His people; it is called the Bible. When God gives His Word to you, it can be trusted. How about you? Can God trust your word? For many the word *commit* is a bad word. When it is used, it is normally diminished by some adjective, like "under commit, over deliver." However, this should not be so with Maximizers. You should say what you mean and do what you say! This is very biblical: *"Let your 'Yes,' be 'Yes,' and your 'No,' 'No,'"* (James 5:12 NKJ). You should be a person who gives your word and keeps your word, especially with God! The biblical term for this is a *vow*. And, as is the case with everything God asks you to do, He prepares a blessing for those who obey, or follow through on, their vows.

As you continue to learn strategic ways to give to God, you cannot neglect the principle of vowing and paying because it has great blessings attached to it. Even before you had an understanding of biblical truths, you implicitly understood this. Do you remember a time when you were in a tough spot and you needed help from God? What did you do? You may have made a promise. You may have said something like, "If you get me out of this, I will do thus and so." And, surprisingly, God came through for you. Did you follow through on your part of the promise? If you did, you found that God honors those who give their word and keep it.

Look at it from Scripture: *"You will pray to him, and he will hear you, and you will fulfill your vows to him. You will succeed in whatever you choose to do, and light will shine on the road ahead of you. If people are in trouble and you say, 'Help them', God will save*

Revolutionary Planting

them" (Job 22:27-29 NLT). This is just one example; but, in precept, it establishes the vow and pay principle.

When you give God your word—make a vow—and you keep it, the Bible says that three blessings occur. First, you will succeed! If you demonstrate that God can trust you, God says, *"You will succeed in whatever you choose to do."* God does not qualify what He says. You will succeed in whatever you do! Therefore, if God knows that He can trust what you say, He will cause you to succeed. Rather than spending a lot of time trying to get people to like you, you should spend more time demonstrating to God that He can trust you. God wants you to succeed, and the vow and pay principle assures this for you. This is a big promise!

You may be asking, "How can I succeed when all I have is an idea but do not know how to enact it?" This is where the second blessing comes in: *"Light will shine on the road ahead of you."* What does light do? It shows you what is ahead. It clarifies what cannot be seen. It ensures that you do not hit hidden obstacles. Having the promise to succeed but no instruction on how to succeed would be a hollow promise. You saw earlier that, when you have clarity of vision, there is acceleration towards the known goal. God gets involved in what you do when He knows He can trust you. God says, in essence, *"I'll show you how to get it done."* With God's leading, you will never go astray and you certainly cannot fail!

Last, God says you can pray for people in trouble and He will save them. Now this is where many people are distracted because they cannot understand how God can make a promise to answer your prayers based on offerings! However, it is very biblical. Look at the example of Solomon: *"That night God appeared to Solomon and said to him, 'Ask for whatever you want me to give you'"* (2 Chronicles

Day 42 - Vow and Pay

1:7 NCV). God gave Solomon a blank check. What made Solomon so special that God would make this type of offer? The answer is found in verse 6: *"Solomon went up to the bronze altar in the presence of the Lord at the Meeting Tent and offered a thousand burnt offerings on it"* (NCV). Solomon brought God a pleasing offering that opened the door to God's generous question. God gave Solomon exactly what he asked for *and* wealth beyond measure. Solomon's offering opened the door for him to ask God for anything.

When you vow to God that you will dedicate something to Him, He believes you and waits for you to keep your word. Once you keep your word by giving what you promised, God gives you the ability to pray for people in perishing predicaments and He will rescue them. Your faithfulness in giving is the catalyst for this.

When God can trust your word, He will show you how to succeed and answer your prayers on behalf of others! Why would you not want these blessings on your life? Now there are those who would say, "I would prefer not to promise and just do it." And that is okay except for the fact that you miss out on the blessings of the vow and pay principle. Think of it this way: You are in school and your teacher says, "If you commit to meet during your lunch break, I will make sure you pass the final exam. But I need to know now if you will come." You say to the teacher, "I can't commit, but I'll try to show up." Do you think that teacher will miss his or her lunch break without a solid commitment? Certainly not! You can still pass the test, but you will have done it without the much-needed help of the instructor.

This is a natural example, and it in no way approximates the seriousness of the commitment that God makes to you when you

Revolutionary Planting

make a promise and keep it. Imagine. You can pray for people in need and God says He will help them. You want this promise operating in you life, don't you?

Jacob promised that, if God would keep him and protect him, Jacob would serve Him and give him a tenth of everything (Genesis 28:20). Jacob found a wife. He became very wealthy and had blessed and prosperous children. And God restored the relationship with his brother, Esau. God even changed his name to Israel, wiping out his past.

Hannah, who was barren, made a vow to God. She promised that, if she bore a child, she would dedicate him completely to the Lord (1 Samuel 1). God answered and Hannah kept her word. As a result, Hannah had more children. Her son, Samuel, became one of the greatest prophets in the nation.

These are just two examples of this principle. But there are many others in scripture. Put this principle to work in your life, and it will maximize your success!

Day 42 - Vow and Pay

Maximized Prayer:
Father, You have always kept Your Word with me! I want You to trust my words so that I can walk in the blessing of the vow and pay principle. In Jesus' name, Amen.

Maximizing Moments:
Have you used this principle before? If not, make a commitment today to God. Vow a certain amount to your church for a Kingdom project, person, or priority. Watch how God moves on your behalf once you pay it.

Maximizing Mantra:
I pay all my vows!

Revolutionary Planting

NOTES

Day 43 – Your Words Matter

"Let us hold fast the confession of our hope without wavering, for he who promised is faithful."
Hebrews 10:23 (ESV)

When you learned about the Faith Process, you were introduced to the importance of words. For the next couple of days, you will gain a greater appreciation for the role your words play in the life you are living today and the life God has promised you. The power of your confession is the catalyst to victory in your Maximized Life. Confession is a statement in agreement with God's Word independent of natural circumstances, situations, and conditions.

In order to live a Maximized Life, you will quickly learn the important principle of maximizing your mouth. Most people are highly developed in victim vocabulary and negative talk. They make excuses why they can't succeed, why people won't help them, and why what they do never seems to succeed. Their speech is punctuated with negatives and self-deprecating words. They have mastered the art of talking themselves out of success. And, when you look at their lives, that's exactly what you see: no success!

If you listen to these people closely, you will hear what they truly believe! Negative speech becomes a self-fulfilling prophecy. The Bible clearly teaches that the words you speak really do matter: *"The tongue can bring death or life; those who love to talk will reap the consequences"* (Proverbs 18:21 NLT). Your words are spiritual containers and have impact. Most people were not taught the dynamic power of the spoken word when they were reared. They did not think that what they said mattered. However, as a spirit being (1 Thessalonians 5:23), when you speak, you affect things in the natural and spiritual realm.

Righteous Proclamations

Jesus taught His disciples that the words people speak are spirit and they are life. Your words set spiritual things in motion. With your words, you transact business in the spiritual realm. As you just read, life and death are in your mouth; and you will reap whatever words you sow. Here is what the Bible says about words:

"By faith, we see the world called into existence by God's word, what we see created by what we don't see." (Hebrews 11:3 MSG)

"It is the Spirit who gives life; the flesh is no help at all. The words that I have spoken to you are spirit and life." (John 6:63 ESV)

"For assuredly, I say to you, whoever says to this mountain, 'Be removed and be cast into the sea,' and does not doubt in his heart, but believes that those things he says will be done, he will have whatever he says." (Mark 11:23 NKJ)

These passages explain the true power of words. Words are very powerful. In Genesis, God creates everything with His Word! The phrase continuously is repeated, *"God said, 'Let there be....'"* Everything that God spoke came to pass and was declared good. Words are spiritual vehicles, and God used them to create the earth.

Your words have that same type of power! The Bible teaches that one who believes that what he or she says will happen, it will come to pass. When you open your mouth, things start to happen.

The first area that your words affect is the spiritual realm. Angels are dispatched in response to your words: "*Bless the LORD, you His angels, Who excel in strength, who do His word, Heeding the voice of His word. Bless the LORD, all you His hosts, You ministers of His, who do His pleasure. Bless the LORD, all His works, In all places of His dominion. Bless the LORD, O my soul*" (Psalm 103:20-22 KJV)! When you speak forth God's Word, angels are on assignment

Day 43 - Your Words Matter

to execute them. Daniel called out to God in prayer. For 21 days, he awaited a response. When the angel appeared, *"Then he said to me, 'Do not fear, Daniel, for from the first day that you set your heart to understand, and to humble yourself before your God, your words were heard; and I have come because of your words'"* (Daniel 10:12 KJV). This is a good reminder to you that, when you are speaking, your words are not just going into empty space. When you say a faith confession, you have set the powers of Heaven into motion.

You should also know that in the same way angels are listening to perform the faith-filled words that you speak, demonic forces are activated or restrained by your words as well. Words spoken in faith release angels and restrain demons. Every evil force is halted by the authoritative, faith-filled words that you speak. Jesus modeled this for the Believer: *"Then the devil led Jesus to the top of a very high mountain and showed him all the kingdoms of the world and all their splendor. The devil said, 'If you will bow down and worship me, I will give you all these things.' Jesus said to the devil, 'Go away from me, satan! It is written in the Scriptures, "You must worship the Lord your God and serve only him."' So the devil left Jesus, and angels came and took care of him"* (Matthew 4:8-11 NCV). Jesus fended off the devil's attack with words. When faith-filled words are spoken from a believing heart, things happen!

On the other hand, fear-filled words restrain angels and release demons. The forces of evil are released when you speak words of doubt and fear, so you must make certain that you never serve as a confirming witness against your future.

Even though confession is important, many Believers start out making confessions of faith but then stop. There are six (6) reasons why Believers stop confessing God's Word. First, when natural circumstances are more real than spiritual truth, some will lose their resolve to continue to speak what God says. Natural circumstances have a voice, and it cries out to them. If that voice drowns out God's voice, they lose their confidence in faith-filled words and start agreeing with their circumstances.

Second, some people are just not comfortable with speaking what their natural eye cannot see! Faith is a lifestyle. If people have not fully embraced the reality of the world—which the eyes cannot see—they will not have a conviction that spiritual forces are listening to what they are saying. (Interestingly enough, these people will still speak negative words and not positive words.)

Third, some think that confessing God's Word will forfeit receiving assistance from others. If someone speaks words of abundance, they may forfeit the help of someone from whom they were hoping to get some money. These people think that "poor mouthing" will produce lasting results. Some will respond to that type of talking, but soon people who speak lack and want will soon be found out; and the help that they desire will not come. Moreover, your words cannot be used to manipulate people! When you make a faith confession over your life, you involve God! God can then work on the heart of a person, and you will not even have to ask! Don't use your words to manipulate people. Use your faith to move God to work on your behalf. He is the best partner to have.

Fourth, some people need acceptance from others who do not understand faith; and they do not make consistent faith confessions. These people are intimidated by the doubts of others. However, your victory by using your mouth will silence all opposition to faith confession. You must hold your course!

Day 43 - Your Words Matter

Fifth, you grow weary in making faith confessions because, in the natural, it appears that nothing is happening. Maximizers are not moved by what they see or what they feel. They are only moved by what they believe. Just because it cannot be seen now does not mean that something isn't happening! You must have faith that heavenly hosts are operating on your behalf—even when you can't see natural progress.

Then, last, some people do not understand the full use of confession. They don't use their mouths as an offensive force to make things happen.

You must realize that your words matter! Start today speaking faith confessions over every area of your life. The spirit world will respond!

Righteous Proclamations

Maximized Prayer:
Father, Your words have power and they are life! I choose to agree with what You have said about me and my future. I cancel every negative word that I've spoken. In Jesus' name, Amen.

Maximizing Moments:
Where are areas in your life that need Maximizing?

Find promises in the Word of God and craft affirmative faith confessions for each one. You should begin to confess these daily. (The Additional Resources Section has a sample of 15 Freedom Truths that you can start with.)

Maximizing Mantra:
I will have what I say.

DAY 44 – THE FORCE OF FAITH

"Truly I tell you, whoever says to this mountain, Be lifted up and thrown into the sea! and does not doubt at all in his heart but believes that what he says will take place, it will be done for him."
Mark 11:23 (AMP)

Yesterday you saw how important your words are. Today you need to understand the power that God wants to release when you speak His Word. Your words are invisible, but they are real and powerful! God has given you the tools to be successful: His Word and your mouth! Many miss out on abundant living because of their mouths. Your words have so much importance that God will hold you accountable for them: *"But I tell you, on the day of judgment men will have to give account for every idle (inoperative, nonworking) word they speak. For by your words you will be justified and acquitted, and by your words you will be condemned and sentenced"* (Matthew 12:36-37 AMP).

Wow! Words are so important that God keeps track of them and will hold you accountable for them. Thus, on an ongoing basis, you have to guard the things that you say. Careless words today can come back to haunt you in the future. You must understand that words are powerful, so take what you say very seriously. You cannot get enmeshed in corrupt communication (words) because your words will work against you. The constant confession out of your mouth will become the present state in which you live.

You must take full advantage of making positive confessions. Here are just a few benefits of your positive confession: satisfaction/fulfillment (Proverbs 18:20), health to your body (Proverbs 12:18), and joy in sad situations (Proverbs 12:25).

Spiritual authority is exercised by the words of your mouth. Even devils must obey what you say: *"When the seventy-two disciples* returned, they joyfully reported to him, 'Lord, even the demons obey us when we use your name'" (Luke 10:17 NLT)! The force of faith can only be released when your heart is established by faith-filled words. What is in your heart will come out of your mouth: *"Good people do good things because of the good in their hearts. Bad people do bad things because of the evil in their hearts. Your words show what is in your heart"* (Luke 6:45 CEV).

Your heart becomes filled with faith-filled words by what you hear: *"So faith comes from hearing, that is, hearing the Good News about Christ"* (Romans 10:17 NLT). As you confess God's Word in addition to God hearing it, you hear it. You are building your faith as you confess God's Word. You are charging yourself with faith as you speak faith-filled words. You may be thinking, "But, as I speak the Words, I am not certain I agree or believe them yet." That's okay! Keep speaking because, as you speak, the force of faith will rise and soon what you are saying will be exactly what you believe. After all, you don't have anything to lose even if you don't believe it right now.

Take, for instance, your finances. You may be in a financial straitjacket. Your bills are behind. Your job is in jeopardy. Your education is limited and the economy is in transition. The farthest thing from your mind is God's promise of abundance. You tremble just trying to say the words: *"The Lord is my shepherd; I have all that I need"* (Psalm 23:1 NLT). But, in point of fact, you have nothing to lose by speaking these words and everything to gain! If you are concerned about what people are going to think, you should know that, if your financial situation deteriorates, they will laugh at you anyway!

Day 44 - The Force of Faith

The doctor may be telling you that your situation is incurable. And everyone that you know who had this same diagnosis has died. Yet you know the Bible says, *"Who his own self bare our sins in his own body on the tree, that we, being dead to sins, should live unto righteousness: by whose stripes ye were healed"* (1 Peter 2:24 KJV). You begin to say, "I believe that, by the stripes of Jesus, I am healed" but stop because you wonder if it's really true. Still speak what God says. Follow the natural order that the doctor gives you, but let the force of faith work on your behalf to do what medicine cannot do!

As you have been exposed to the Maximized Life, much of what you have learned may seem strange—down right unbelievable—based upon where you are. However, if you will keep on saying what God says, the force of faith will bring you everything that you have read about the Maximized Life. You just need to sow the Word into your heart!

Look at this parable that Jesus taught: *"The farmer plants the Word. Some people are like the seed that falls on the hardened soil of the road. No sooner do they hear the Word than Satan snatches away what has been planted in them. And some are like the seed that lands in the gravel. When they first hear the Word, they respond with great enthusiasm. But there is such shallow soil of character that when the emotions wear off and some difficulty arrives, there is nothing to show for it. The seed cast in the weeds represents the ones who hear the kingdom news but are overwhelmed with worries about all the things they have to do and all the things they want to get. The stress strangles what they heard, and nothing comes of it. But the seed planted in the good earth represents those who hear the Word, embrace it, and produce a harvest beyond their wildest dreams"* (Mark 4:14-20 MSG).

Righteous Proclamations

Many have thought that the sower is the pastor who teaches the Word of God. But that is not accurate. You are the farmer. Think about it. A farmer cannot get a harvest by planting seed in another's field. He can only plant in his own field. Therefore, it is not enough for you to hear the Word taught week after week. If you take the lessons taught and intentionally plant them in your heart through repetitious information, you will cultivate the force of faith. And, as you speak, you will see results quickly.

You should keep making your confessions even when results cannot be seen. Keep confessing you will move from disbelief to belief. As you sow the Word in your heart, you will drive out doubt; and the confidence that comes from faith will encompass you. You will keep going from level to level. Now things in the natural will start obeying you. They didn't start obeying you, but now the force of faith is flowing. You will have what you say!

Maximized Prayer:
Father, I believe Your report for my life. I accept Your Word for my life. I believe. Help my unbelief. In Jesus' name, Amen.

Maximizing Moments:
Start diligently making your confessions of faith that you wrote yesterday. (Notice where you have mental resistance to what you are confessing. Don't stop confessing; the force of faith will rise.)

Maximizing Mantra:
I have what you say I have. I am who you say I am.

Day 45 – The Word Works

"But we continue to preach because we have the same kind of faith the psalmist had when he said, 'I believed in God, so I spoke.'"
2 Corinthians 4:13 (NLT)

As you learned, a faith confession is a verbal statement in agreement with the will of God regardless of the circumstances. Do not get intimidated by what your circumstances look like. Make the quality decision to release the force of faith by saying what God says. As you learned yesterday, you can keep on speaking until you believe. And, once you believe, you must keep on speaking.

Your faith will be built today as you see more examples from Scripture: *"When Abram was ninety-nine years old, the Lord appeared to him and said, 'I am God Almighty. Obey me and do what is right. I will make an agreement between us, and I will make you the ancestor of many people.' Then Abram bowed facedown on the ground. God said to him, 'I am making my agreement with you: I will make you the father of many nations. I am changing your name from Abram to Abraham because I am making you a father of many nations'"* (Genesis 17:1-5 NCV).

God changed Abram's name to Abraham, which means, "father of many nations." When God changed his name, Abraham was not the father of any. But God said he is the father of many. God did not tell him that he *will be* the father of many. He *is* the father of many. Every time someone called Abraham's name, they were confessing over him. When God spoke these words, He was setting Abraham's destiny in order: *"We call Abraham 'father' not because he got God's attention by living like a saint, but because God made something out of Abraham when he was a nobody. Isn't that what we've always read in Scripture, God saying to Abraham, 'I set you up as father of many peoples'? Abraham was first named 'father' and then became a father because he dared to trust God to do what only God could do: raise the dead to life, with a word make something out of nothing. When everything was hopeless, Abraham believed anyway, deciding to live not on the basis of what he saw he couldn't do but on what God said he would do. And so he was made father of a multitude of peoples. God himself said to him, 'You're going to have a big family, Abraham'"* (Romans 4:17-18 MSG)!

Later in Genesis, God changed Sarai's name to Sarah for the same reason. When people met them and they introduced themselves, they were speaking their destinies!

Can you rehearse what God has said about you even when you cannot see it? Can you call yourself blessed even when all around you does not look blessed? Can you call yourself abundantly supplied when your needs are not met? You must develop the discipline (enforced obedience) to speak over your life what God has said before you will see the manifestation.

Look at the life of John the Baptist. John knew he had a purpose for his life. He knew that he was to be the forerunner for the Messiah, Jesus Christ. People came out into the wilderness to see him and hear his message. When they asked him who he was, he did not say, "Hi, my name is John": *"John told them in the words of the prophet Isaiah: 'I am the voice of one calling out in the desert: "Make the road straight for the Lord"* (John 1:23 NCV). John identified himself by what Scripture said about him. He could have said his name and he would have been accurate. But he knew that destiny was before him. He had to speak forth exactly what God said he would be. And he did!

Jesus did the same thing. When He introduced His public ministry, He identified Himself with what the Scriptures said about

Day 45 - The Word Works

Him: *"The book of Isaiah the prophet was given to him. He opened the book and found the place where this is written: 'The Lord has put his Spirit in me, because he appointed me to tell the Good News to the poor. He has sent me to tell the captives they are free and to tell the blind that they can see again* (Isaiah 61:1). *God sent me to free those who have been treated unfairly* (Isaiah 58:6) *and to announce the time when the Lord will show his kindness'* (Isaiah 61:2). *Jesus closed the book, gave it back to the assistant, and sat down. Everyone in the synagogue was watching Jesus closely"* (Luke 4:17-20 NCV). While everyone marveled at Jesus, He made a bold declaration: *"You've just heard Scripture make history. It came true just now in this place"* (v. 21 MSG).

Jesus had not performed any miracles. He had not multiplied anyone's lunch. He did not even have any followers. Yet He had the boldness to declare who He is and what He was sent to do. He concluded by telling them that right now this Scripture is true. Not tomorrow or the next day. It is true now!

If your confessions are going to be meaningful, they will need to be simple and personal; and they need to be in the present tense and in agreement with God's Word. Your tongue will write the script for your life and determine your destiny. If you have crafted confessions that are in the future tense, revise them now! Because *"faith is the substance of things hoped for, the evidence of things not seen"* (Hebrews 11:1 NKJ). Faith is always present tense. If it is anything other than present tense, it is not faith.

Once you have made your confession, you must maintain confidence in your confession: *"Do not, therefore, fling away your fearless confidence, for it carries a great and glorious compensation of reward"* (Hebrews 10:35 AMP). Remain confident in spite of what you see. It is only temporary. The eternal Word of God is changing things around you even when you cannot see it! Trust the process. You should have confidence because you know who you are from the Word of God and you know the Truth about your situation and not just the facts.

Confession is like a lay-away plan. When you understand all that God has made available through His Word, you confess His Word over your life. You believe you receive it when you pray. At that moment, the angel of God goes into His storehouse and tags for you whatever you confessed and believed you received when you prayed. It is now designated and set aside for you. However, though it is yours, you still have to make the payments before you can see it. The words that you speak out of your mouth are the lay-away payments. Each day, multiple times a day, as you speak His Word, you bring those items closer and closer to manifestation. Although you have no physical evidence, you have a claim check. Your claim check is the Bible! One day, before you know it, all your payments (confession) will have been made and what you have believed for will show up! Confession works because *"that's how it is with my (God's) words. They don't return to me without doing everything I send them to do"* (Isaiah 55:11 CEV).

Here is what happens when you speak forth God's Word:

- You release faith in the earth.
- Satanic forces are stopped.
- You release the creative power of God in the earth.
- You transact business in the spirit realm.
- You give God something to confirm in your life.
- You declare what you actually believe in your heart.

- You place your order for what you desire for your life.
- You release angels to go to work on your behalf.

You have something to say about your life! Say what God's Word says because the Word always works.

Maximized Prayer:
Father, You have called me blessed. You have called me healed. You have called me whole! I receive all this and expect manifestation in Jesus' name, Amen.

Maximizing Moments:
Check your heart today. What is the major input? Are you spending more time listening to fear-filled words or faith-filled words?

Find someone who can be an accountability partner as it relates to your words. Have them keep you aware of negative, fear-filled words.

Maximizing Mantra:
I am a Maximizer and every area of my life is blessed!

Notes

Day 46 – Don't Give Up

*"Never give up. Eagerly follow the Holy Spirit
and serve the Lord."*
Romans 12:11 (CEV)

You have learned a lot of information over the past 45 days. In this last week, you will be encouraged to synthesize and internalize what you have learned so that it becomes a natural part of your life. By virtue of the fact that you have made it this far in the journey, you have demonstrated a significant amount of persistence. Persistence is the quality of continuing steadily despite problems or difficulties. In order to do this, there must be resolve. Resolve is arriving at a firm conviction about something with a commitment to a definite course of action!

Many people give up at the first sight of a challenge. After completing this journey, you should be encouraged every time you witness a "reversal." You may ask why? It's because, as a Maximizer, you understand how to overcome any problem or challenge that faces you or will ever face you. What you need to possess now is persistence. Being able to stick with the process until successful completion!

This ability to stay the course only comes when there is a resolve of persistence. You must say to yourself, "I will not be defeated and I will not quit! I win every faith fight and I don't stop until I win." When you demonstrate that you have the resolve of persistence, *"Then we will no longer be immature like children. We won't be tossed and blown about by every wind of new teaching. We will not be influenced when people try to trick us with lies so clever they sound like the truth. Instead, we will speak the truth in love, growing in every way more and more like Christ, who is the head of his body, the church. He makes the whole body fit together perfectly. As each part does its own special work, it helps the other parts grow, so that the whole body is healthy and growing and full of love"* (Ephesians 4:14-17 NLT). No one else can do what you have been assigned to do; this is why you must have persistence to accomplish the task that is set before you.

You should cultivate the internal motivation to accomplish every task with persistence: *"So, dear brothers and sisters, work hard to prove that you really are among those God has called and chosen. Do these things, and you will never fall away"* (2 Peter 1:10 NLT). This sounds like persistence. The blessing is that, when you develop a resolve of persistence, it guarantees the maximum return on your efforts. When this is accomplished, there is a belief system modification that takes place. You no longer do just enough to get by or what is required. You go the extra mile. When this takes place, you position yourself for peace, power, and prosperity. Living in harmony with God and man, you begin to live life with the absence of agitation and discord. The power comes from the confidence in the thing that God has spoken and performed by His Word. The prosperity comes from the increase that is placed on your life by doing more than the average that is required: *"Therefore, my beloved brethren, be firm (steadfast), immovable, always abounding in the work of the Lord [always being superior, excelling, doing more than enough in the service of the Lord], knowing and being continually aware that your labor in the Lord is not futile [it is never wasted or to no purpose]"* (1 Corinthians 15:58, AMP).

To develop this resolve, there is a process to which you must submit. You have learned a lot about process; so you understand that, if you live out the process, it will produce results for you. The end result will produce victory in your life: *"And he said, 'So is the*

Day 46 - Don't Give Up

kingdom of God, as if a man should cast seed into the ground; And should sleep, and rise night and day, and the seed should spring and grow up, he knoweth not how. For the earth bringeth forth fruit of herself; first the blade, then the ear, after that the full corn in the ear. But when the fruit is brought forth, immediately he putteth in the sickle, because the harvest is come'" (Mark 4: 26-29 KJV). This Scripture affirms that if you respect the process, even though you do not understand it completely, there will be a great harvest.

This process begins with ***Consecration.*** When you decide to live for God exclusively and to fulfill His purposes in the earth, you are consecrated to His service. This is fundamental to the process because if you are not "sold out" to God and His Word, you will waver based on what you determine to be truth at that moment. You were set apart for God through salvation, and your choice to stay separated is called consecration.

The next step in the process is ***Separation.*** Once you have been consecrated and you have a compass to determine right and wrong, you will need to judge everything around you to see if it fits with your consecrated status. You will have to detach yourself from any thing and anyone that interferes with your destiny.

After separation, you should pursue the proper ***Information.*** This is an ongoing pursuit: *"My people will be destroyed, because they have no knowledge. You have refused to learn, so I will refuse to let you be priests to me. You have forgotten the teachings of your God, so I will forget your children"* (Hosea 4:6 NCV). This biblical information will guide your life and will provide dividends even to future generations.

Once you possess information, you must not settle for a casual acquaintance with it. As you have seen, the best way to build the resolve of persistence is hearing the Word of God on a daily basis.

Resolve of Persistence

This is the process called **Saturation**. Saturation is the intentional immersion into information to the degree that mental transformation takes place. This is not a quick process. (This is why you are encouraged to listen to Bible teachings at least 1 hour a day). The more you acquire the information needed to Maximize Your Life and saturate yourself with it, the more you will build a fortress of internal resolve that will carry you through every storm and will not be easily penetrated!

Next you will need **Deliberation**. At this stage in the process, you will make conscious choices to do those things that cause you to grow. Studying the Word of God is a fundamental discipline that the Maximizer needs. This deliberation gives you a continual source of information, which leads to your transformation. Determination will build as you exercise discipline over your flesh (sinful desires). The quickest way to break your resolve of persistence is by a lack of discipline (enforced obedience). There will be days when you do not feel like following through on your commitments or this process. This is where you must enforce obedience on yourself and keep going. Determination long term will build expectation. You anticipate that everything God has promised will come to pass.

A word that can be interchangeably used with persistence is faithfulness. When you are found faithful, there are blessings that are in store for you. You may know people whose lives you admire. But admiration is not enough. You must be willing to persevere in order to see your dreams fulfilled. You must be proven faithful. Can God trust you with more? Are you faithful to the things of God? Do you hang in there when the going gets tough?

You may not be able to answer yes to these questions, but that is okay: *"If my people, which are called by my name, shall humble*

Day 46 - Don't Give Up

themselves, and pray, and seek my face, and turn from their wicked ways; then will I hear from heaven, and will forgive their sin, and will heal their land" (2 Chronicles 7:14, KJV). If you change your ways and repent, you will get back in line to receive the manifested blessings for which you have been waiting. Notice "back in line" is not to the back of the line. The beautiful thing about God is that, when you repent, God restores and refreshes you: *"Repent therefore and be converted, that your sins may be blotted out, so that times of refreshing may come from the presence of the Lord"* (Act 3:19 NKJ). Get rid of all that extra baggage of unforgiveness that you are carrying. It makes your Maximized Life Journey more difficult. Just don't quit!

Maximized Prayer:
Father, I thank You for finishing grace in every area of my life. May I be found faithful to You and the Maximized Life Journey that I am on. In Jesus' name, Amen.

Maximizing Moments:
Review the process you learned today. Where are you in this process? Where did this process breakdown?

Reflect on the times you have lost your discipline and given up. List the things that distract you. Was it a lack of saturation? Determination? Expectation?

Maximizing Mantra:
I never quit!

DAY 47 – BE DILIGENT

"But without faith it is impossible to please and be satisfactory to Him. For whoever would come near to God must [necessarily] believe that God exists and that He is the rewarder of those who earnestly and diligently seek Him [out]."
Hebrews 11:6 (AMP)

Diligence produces results and is very important to God. Diligence is the purposeful, calculated pursuit of consistency to hold one's course; it is maximum, sustained effort based on your commitment to God; a deliberate, calculated effort to accomplish a task. Persons are found diligent when they willingly exhaust all possibilities. A person who is diligent views life from a different perspective. Giving up is not an option. A diligent person will find a way to make it work!

Diligence is God's order to keep you faithful, fruitful, and focused. With this, you will never fail or fall. Diligence has several character traits. Today you should examine yourself to see if you have the characteristics of a diligent person.

It all starts with your attitude. You have to check your attitude because "your attitude determines your altitude." In other words, you will only go as high as your attitude will take you. Many people, when they are doing their jobs, have bad attitudes; and this is why promotion and pay increases evade them. Did you know that a good attitude can get you noticed and cause you to find favor in uncommon places with uncommon people? The most unlikely persons will use their power, their influence, and their abilities to make things happen for you when you have a good attitude.

You have to change your attitude about work: *"For we are God's [own] handiwork (His workmanship), recreated in Christ Jesus, [born*

Resolve of Persistence

anew] that we may do those good works which God predestined (planned beforehand) for us [taking paths which He prepared ahead of time], that we should walk in them [living the good life which He prearranged and made ready for us to live]" (Ephesians 2:10 AMP). God created you to work! Work is God's plan to bring the internal potential out of you in order to produce maximum productivity. You should change your language concerning work because you will always have what you say. If you say, "My job is killing me," then it will.

Diligence does not mean working harder but working smarter, being more efficient. When you work smarter, you will not always have to be the most effective. However, once your process is completed, you will have discovered the most effective means to complete every task. When you have been diligent in work, then you are rewarded with rest. A person who rests without work is a robber and a thief. You have robbed yourself of reaching your maximum potential, and you have robbed others who were counting on you to do your part. Christ set the example for you: *"We must work the works of Him Who sent Me and be busy with His business while it is daylight; night is coming on, when no man can work"* (John 9:4 AMP).

Diligence is signified by a balanced life. Here is where a lot of people miss it. There is an order that God has placed in the earth to keep us balanced. God first, family second, work third, and everyone else fights for fourth. In a balanced life, you will never put anything before your relationship with God. Keeping Him first will keep you focused and diligent. Diligence does not sacrifice family for any reason—period! Years ago, people were misled into thinking that you should put your work before your family. That is not the order

Day 47 - Be Diligent

of God. And order is important to God: *"For because you did not do it the first time, the LORD our God broke out against us, because we did not consult Him about the proper order"* (I Chronicles 15:13 NKJ). You cannot violate God's order and expect to complete the Maximized Life Journey. Your activities are to glorify God. You cannot give honor to God if your life is out of order.

Consistency is the next character trait. You cannot have a wavering spirit: *"But when you ask him, be sure that your faith is in God alone. Do not waver, for a person with divided loyalty is as unsettled as a wave of the sea that is blown and tossed by the wind. Such people should not expect to receive anything from the Lord. Their loyalty is divided between God and the world, and they are unstable in everything they do"* (James 1:6-8 NLT). Consistency is very important. It proves that you can be counted on. If you are not consistent in your behaviors, you will hinder your journey.

Then you must demonstrate determination. You must build an inner resolve to finish. You should associate a great deal of pain with not finishing. Find areas where you have not finished and have become comfortable with failure. Quit once and it's easier to quit again and again. God has an assignment for your life. He expects you to finish it. Jesus had an assignment and He finished it. Paul had an assignment and He finished it. You have an assignment. Will you finish it? God has dispatched sufficient grace to help you complete your assignment.

Last, *diligence is characterized by excellence.* Excellence pays attention to detail that gives birth to superior performance, which causes maximized potential, promotion in life, and praise to God. Excellence may cost more, but it always pays for itself. Excellence requires exposure. You cannot aspire to a level of superior

Resolve of Persistence

performance to which you have not been exposed. Excellence always attracts. Excellence is not what you do, but who you are. Excellence must be pursued for the pleasure and praise of God. The desire and passion to develop excellence must outweigh the pain and discomfort caused by change; otherwise, the attempt to establish excellence will be aborted by disgruntled others. The reason for development of excellence is above and beyond natural reward and human praise. Again, excellence costs but it pays for itself. The conditions that you are willing to tolerate speak volumes about who you really are. To walk in excellence, you must abandon all excuses for a mediocre lifestyle. Excuses are crutches for the uncommitted and incompetent.

Your diligence will show itself in the character traits you demonstrate. Be diligent!

Maximized Prayer:
Father, thank You for the examples of diligence that I find in Your Word. Please keep me focused and unwavering in my pursuit of the Maximized Life. In Jesus' name, Amen.

Maximizing Moments:
What does excellence look like in your life?
What can you do today to raise the level of excellence in every area of your life?

Maximizing Mantra:
I am found diligent in all things!

Day 48 – No More Excuses

"But they all with one accord began to make excuses. The first said to him, 'I have bought a piece of ground, and I must go and see it. I ask you to have me excused.'"
Luke 14:18 (NKJ)

Excuses will rob from you what God has prepared for you! There is an importance and power in excuse-free living. If you will be a diligent person who overcomes everything in life, you must eliminate all excuses!

Look at the entire parable that is used for our reading today: *"Jesus replied with this story: 'A man prepared a great feast and sent out many invitations. When the banquet was ready, he sent his servant to tell the guests, "Come, the banquet is ready." But they all began making excuses. One said, "I have just bought a field and must inspect it. Please excuse me." Another said, "I have just bought five pairs of oxen, and I want to try them out. Please excuse me." Another said, "I now have a wife, so I can't come." The servant returned and told his master what they had said. His master was furious and said, "Go quickly into the streets and alleys of the town and invite the poor, the crippled, the blind, and the lame." After the servant had done this, he reported, "There is still room for more." So his master said, "Go out into the country lanes and behind the hedges and urge anyone you find to come, so that the house will be full. For none of those I first invited will get even the smallest taste of my banquet'"* (Luke 14:16-24 NLT).

A feast was prepared and personal invitations were issued. Yet all those who had been invited manufactured excuses for their absence! Today you should gain the resolve to reject any and all excuses so that you can live the life of an overcomer that has been prepared for you by Jesus Christ. Life is choice driven and you can choose how

Resolve of Persistence

you will respond. When you look at the excuses in the parable above, none of them is compelling. As a Maximizer, you cannot hide behind an excuse.

An excuse is a fabricated reason to abandon your resolve, to avoid repentance, to abdicate your responsibility, to authenticate your representations, or to apologize for your resources. Excuse making is when you compromise under pressure. It is a lack of integrity within your heart–lack of boldness—to face whatever ridicule you will have to face. So why do people make excuses?

People make excuses when

- they are asked to do things that they don't want to do,
- they give their word and they don't want to keep it,
- they should make necessary changes and they don't want to,
- they know they are wrong and don't want to admit it, or
- they choose to apologize for the favor of God on their life.

You do not have to live with excuse making in your life. Once and for all, develop a winning attitude and approach to life; this is what the Maximized Life Journey is all about. Everything that you have been given because of the New Birth in Christ is yours. Your personal, professional, and spiritual growth is at stake when you choose to make excuses. Most people are highly developed in excuse making. And excuses are smoke screens because those who are paying attention can see right through them.

Look at some famous excuses in the Bible. God approached Gideon to serve as a deliverer for Israel in order to bring them out from Midianite domination. God told Gideon what He was prepared to do. Gideon responded by making excuses: *"But Lord,'*

Day 48 - No More Excuses

Gideon replied, 'how can I rescue Israel? My clan is the weakest in the whole tribe of Manasseh, and I am the least in my entire family' (Judges 6:15 NLT)! When God spoke to Peter about launching out into the deep to catch fish, his first response was to make an excuse: *"Simon said, 'Master, we've been fishing hard all night and haven't caught even a minnow'"* (Luke 5:5 MSG). God approached a man who was lame for 28 years. He asked the man if he wanted to be healed. The man replied, *"Sir, there is no one to help me get into the pool when the water starts moving. While I am coming to the water, someone else always gets in before me"* (John 5:7 NCV). In each of these situations, excuses were used as shields to maintain the status quo.

As a Maximizer, you must rise above the initial temptation to cover yourself and miss God's abundant plan for your life. Your excuses become a crutch to hide your lack of commitment, and they sabotage your response during the difficult times so that you forfeit your reward. Excuses cancel next-level functioning and maintain stagnancy in your life. Excuses will rob you of the joy of discovering unexpected help from God and the ordained resources that He has already arranged.

At key points in your life, you will have a choice to stand firm or make excuses. Stand firm and see the hand of God work on your behalf: *"There is no longer Jew or Gentile, slave or free, male and female. For you are all one in Christ Jesus. And now that you belong to Christ, you are the true children of Abraham. You are his heirs, and God's promise to Abraham belongs to you"* (Galatians 3:28-29 NLT).

At this point in your journey, you cannot reject what God has promised you! God has promised you abundant life and you cannot accept anything less; moreover, you cannot make excuses as to why

Resolve of Persistence

His promises are not manifested in your life. It's not because of your gender, your education, your heritage, or your place of birth. You are entitled to the Maximized Life, and you should not make any excuses for not living it. You have come too far in this journey! Everything God has assigned for you, He will make it happen if you rid yourself of excuses.

So why do people make excuses?

- The fear of failure and rejection
- The unawareness of unrecognizable resources
- A sense of inferiority
- Staying in your comfort zone
- Unwillingness to challenge accepted norms
- Pride and exalted thinking
- Being tired and exhausted

God loves you too much to allow your excuses to remain. You have learned how to recondition your thinking and how the way you present yourself tells others about Who God is. If you live your life by excuses, you will misrepresent the God you serve!

As it relates to excuses, you must identify the stage at which you are prone to quit and rationalize your failure through a well-thought out excuse. The time wasted crafting an excuse can be better spent solving the problem!

Make excuses a thing of the past. Never feel comfortable living your life by excuses. You are better than that and God expects more. With the conviction that you are a winner, you can win with the hand you have been dealt. You have been called to win. All you need is a commitment to win. The faith fight that you are in is fixed! You will win if you reject excuses, keep living by faith and giving it your all.

Maximized Prayer:

> Father, I reject the excuse making habits of the past. I will trust You to keep Your Word, and I will do my part and obey You in all things. In Jesus' name, Amen.

Maximizing Moments:

> What excuses have you lived by? In what areas of your life have you become accustomed to excuses for less than stellar progress?
>
> What is your plan to overcome these excuses so that you can maximize these areas of your life?

Maximizing Mantra:
> I am destined to win in life!

Notes

DAY 49 – MAXIMIZING YOUR PRAISE

"Enter with the password: 'Thank you!'
Make yourselves at home, talking praise.
Thank him. Worship him."
Psalm 100:4 (MSG)

Most Believers will agree that praising God and being thankful is good; though it is good, many think it is optional. If they don't want to do it, they just don't. Still others only praise God when their circumstances are good and everything is going their way. These people think that praising God is only response to what has actually happened. Yet there are others who only make time to praise God in sudden downturns and reversals. When life is good, they go about life not acknowledging God. But as soon as something goes wrong, they run to God and begin to thank Him for all that He has done in the past in an effort to motivate God to help them in their current situation. None of these behaviors is acceptable to God. The truth is that praising God is not an option.

The effects of praise are tremendous on the Sovereign, satan, and the saint (Believer). The purpose and value of praise in the life of the Believer cannot be underestimated. For the next 2 days, you will gain a greater appreciation of the purpose and power of praise. You will leave these 2 days convinced that praise should not be another activity but rather a lifestyle. As a Maximizer, you'll find that praise is a tool that will propel you to the place of your destiny.

Praise is a vocal expression of love, adoration, and appreciation to God. You should praise God in everything. All Believers are commanded to praise God: *"I have made Israel for myself, and they will someday honor me before the whole world"* (Isaiah 43:21 NLT). One of your primary reasons to exist is to praise God: *"Through Him, therefore, let us constantly and at all times offer up to God a*

Radical Praise

sacrifice of praise, which is the fruit of lips that thankfully acknowledge and confess and glorify His name" (Hebrews 13:15 AMP). Since we have been created and commanded by God to praise Him, it is not optional. Psalm 150 (NKJ) puts it this way: *"Let everything that has breath praise the LORD. Praise the LORD!"*

So the first reason why you should praise God is because you have been created and commanded to do it: *"In everything give thanks: for this is the will of God in Christ Jesus concerning you"* (I Thessalonians 5:18 NKJ). In fact, you should offer the sacrifice of praise to God continually, which is the fruit of your lips: *"In Christ we were chosen to be God's people, because from the very beginning God had decided this in keeping with his plan. And he is the One who makes everything agree with what he decides and wants. We are the first people who hoped in Christ, and we were chosen so that we would bring praise to God's glory"* (Ephesians 1:11-12 NCV).

Praise is not automatic; it is a deliberate act and a calculated choice that empowers you to stand while you are waiting for what you believe you received when you prayed. Praise is one of your spiritual weapons that originates in a heart full of love toward God: *"So love the LORD your God with all your heart, soul, and strength"* (Deuteronomy 6:5 CEV). Our response to God's directive to praise should then be obeyed: *"If you love me, obey my commandments"* (John 14:15 NLT).

Another reason why you should praise God is because it glorifies Him: *"With all my heart I will praise you, O Lord my God. I will give glory to your name forever, for your love for me is very great. You have rescued me from the depths of death"* (Psalm 86:12-13 NLT). Moreover, praise gives you the opportunity to bless the Lord: *"BLESS (AFFECTIONATELY, gratefully praise) the Lord, O my*

Day 49 - Maximizing Your Praise

soul! O Lord my God, You are very great! You are clothed with honor and majesty" (Psalm 104:1 AMP).

Finally, praise fortifies your spirit man: *"Why are you cast down, O my soul? And why are you disquieted within me? Hope in God; For I shall yet praise Him, The help of my countenance and my God"* (Psalm 43:5 NKJ).

So how do you praise God? Praise is possible when you focus on Who He is to you. From sincere reflection, you will be able to proclaim that God's goodness, which is without measure, is abundant and overflowing! Here are some ways to get started: Praise God for His holiness, mercy, and justice (2 Chronicles 20:21; Psalm 99:3-4). Praise God for His grace (Ephesians 1:6). Praise Him for His goodness (Psalm 135:3). Praise God for His kindness (Psalm 117). Praise God for His salvation (Ephesians 2:8-9). You can praise God without limits, anywhere and anytime.

Praise to God can be offered freely and over time; it will be as normal as taking a breath. Sometimes you praise God privately: *"I will be glad and rejoice in you; I will sing praise to your name, O Most High"* (Psalm 9:2 NKJ). Other times you have the opportunity to give glory and praise to our God publicly: *"I will declare your name to my brothers; in the congregation I will praise you"* (Psalm 22:22 NLT). Search out opportunities to bring praise to God!

Praising and worshiping God is done in many different positions and forms. Here are several biblical examples:

Sitting: *"When the day of Pentecost came, they were all together in one place. Suddenly a noise like a strong, blowing wind came from heaven and filled the whole house where they were sitting."* (Acts 2:1-2 NCV)

Radical Praise

Kneeling: *"Come, let us bow down in worship, let us kneel before the LORD our Maker."* (Psalm 95:6 NLT)

Standing: *"Whenever the people saw the pillar of cloud standing at the entrance to the tent, they all stood and worshiped, each at the entrance to his tent."* (Exodus 33:10 NCV)

Lying prostrate/bowing down: *"And when all the people saw it, they fell on their faces and said, 'The LORD, he is God; the LORD, he is God.'"* (1 Kings 18:39 ESV)

"Ezra praised the LORD, the great God; and all the people lifted their hands and responded, 'Amen! Amen!' Then they bowed down and worshiped the LORD with their faces to the ground." (Nehemiah 8:6 AMP)

Bowing head: *"Moreover King Hezekiah and the leaders commanded the Levites to sing praise to the LORD with the words of David and of Asaph the seer. So they sang praises with gladness, and they bowed their heads and worshiped."* (2 Chronicles 29:30 NKJ)

Lifting hands: *"Thus will I bless thee while I live: I will lift up my hands in thy name."* (Psalm 63:4 KJV)

Dancing: *"Praise his name with dancing, accompanied by tambourine and harp."* (Psalm 149:3 NLT)

Praise to God is designed to be expressive and heartfelt! Do not be restricted as you demonstrate praise to your God!

Maximized Prayer:
Father, I will praise You regardless of the circumstances in my life. You are worthy to be praised every moment of every day. In Jesus' name, Amen.

Maximizing Moments:
For what are you thankful? Write it down and begin today to praise God for it.

Offer the sacrifice of praise for those things that you are still in faith for. Praise God like they have already happened and soon they will manifest.

Maximizing Mantra:
I will bless the Lord at all times and His praise shall continually be in my mouth.

Notes

Day 50 – A Lifestyle of Praise

*"Therefore, let us offer through Jesus
a continual sacrifice of praise to God,
proclaiming our allegiance to his name."*
Hebrews 13:14 (NLT)

Praise to God is expressed outwardly through your everyday actions as well as your words. In all you do, your desire should be to bring glory and honor to God.

So how can you bring praise to God? What can you do to make it an integral part of your life? Praise can be expressed in song, in verse, or in prayer; and it should be done continuously:

"I will bless the LORD at all times: his praise shall continually be in my mouth." (Psalm 34:1 KJV)

"Upon You have I leaned and relied from birth; You are He Who took me from my mother's womb and You have been my benefactor from that day. My praise is continually of You." (Psalm 71:6 AMP)

There are ways to make praise a part of your daily life. It is possible to praise God in any place and at any time of the day. Living a life full of praise can assist you in becoming who God wants you to be. Praise is not influenced by how you feel; rather, it is an act of your will while you choose to be thankful for everything that God has done and promised.

Thanksgiving and praise are initiated by each person and can determine the strength of your relationship with God. Your attitude, then, should be one of thankfulness regardless of how you feel. Now, remember, in a relationship, there are benefits; and, with God, there are several benefits to committed praise. First, it stops the enemy. When the enemy tries with all his might to distract, discourage, and ultimately kill your spirit, praise brings a sense of

Radical Praise

God's presence on the scene. There are examples in the Bible of enemies arrayed to destroy God's people: *"The Israelites arose and went up to the house of God [Bethel] and asked counsel of God and said, Which of us shall take the lead to battle against the Benjamites? And the Lord said, Judah shall go up first"* (Judges 20:18 AMP). Yet God intervened at the sound of praise.

Second, praise releases you from emotional bondage and from the pain of your past. Realistically, there are situations in life that bring pain. You may have even lived through painful, traumatic episodes; yet, as you intentionally praise God, you drive away all doubt, fear, anger, and depression because praise invites God's presence into your life. As His presence invades your life, pain is driven far from you.

Third, praise brings deliverance. See the story of Paul and Silas when they were unfairly imprisoned: *"Around midnight Paul and Silas were praying and singing hymns to God, and the other prisoners were listening. Suddenly, there was a massive earthquake, and the prison was shaken to its foundations. All the doors immediately flew open, and the chains of every prisoner fell off"* (Acts 16:25-26 NLT). When you feel like all your options are exhausted, turn to praising God and watch Him break through a wall for you!

Last, praise causes God to defend your rights. Throughout the Book of Psalms, cries are made to God through praise! As the psalmist praised God, God arose to judge his accusers and defend his rights. God will do the same for you. Praise declares your total dependence on God. He must get involved in your affairs and bring you protect you. Every time God gets involved, it triggers His supernatural power: *"But thou art holy, O thou that inhabitest the praises of Israel"* (Psalm 22:3 KJV). When God shows up, His power

Day 50 - A Lifestyle of Praise

is dispatched on your behalf. Praise gets God's attention and causes an immediate response. Let your life be filled with continual praise to God.

David's life was filled with this continual praise to God. Through every phase of his life, praise was the hallmark of David's life. When he wrote Psalm 71, he was an old man who had been in many dangers and difficulties while serving God. He had been rescued from his own sins on more than one occasion. When he thought of the faithfulness of God and how God had blessed him, he said, *"I have relied on you from the day I was born. You brought me safely through birth, and I always praise you"* (Psalm 71:6 CEV). As he thought over all this, he determined to praise God even more than he had in the past. He exhorted himself saying, *"And I praise and honor you all day long"* (Psalm 71:8 KJV). He determined that *"I will never give up hope or stop praising you"* (v. 14).

However, the most fundamental of all reasons to praise God is simply for Who He is. David recognized this in the well-known Psalm 103. In this psalm, David praised God for His many blessings: *"Bless the LORD, O my soul; And all that is within me, bless His holy name! Bless the LORD, O my soul, And forget not all His benefits"* (vv. 1-2 NKJ). Then, he went on to list the wonderful blessings that can come only from the hand of God. But, even before David began to bless God for all His blessings, he started this song of praise with a declaration of Who God is! Before David praised God for what He had done, he praised God for Who He is!

Not only should the Lord continually be praised for His work in creating the universe and humanity, but He should also be praised for His works of deliverance. More times than you are aware, you have been delivered from danger and destruction. You are constantly

Radical Praise

faced with dangers both seen and unseen. That's cause for you to open your mouth and praise Him: *"If God hadn't been for us—all together now, Israel, sing out!—If God hadn't been for us when everyone went against us, We would have been swallowed alive by their violent anger, Swept away by the flood of rage, drowned in the torrent; We would have lost our lives in the wild, raging water"* (Psalm 124:1-2 MSG).

You should also praise God for the relationship you have with Him through the blood of our Lord Jesus Christ. Be thankful for restoring fellowship between you and Him when that fellowship has been broken by your own sin. God always gives you a recovery plan when you mess up your relationship with Him. You should praise Him for this awesome Journey that you are on to reach your highest potential for the Kingdom of God! Praising God will make the Journey go faster!

Maximized Prayer:

Father, I love You with all my heart. I appreciate who You are and the many doors that You have opened for me. I will rejoice and be glad. In Jesus' name, Amen.

Maximizing Moments:

In what areas of your life do you need God to show up? Begin today to praise God consistently and intentionally over those areas.

How often do you praise God? Praise should be as natural to you as breathing. Be more intentional about praising every where and at all times.

Maximizing Mantra:

This is the day the Lord has made, and I will rejoice and be glad in it!

NOTES

Day 51 – Maximizers on a Mission

*"For promotion cometh neither from the east,
nor from the west, nor from the south.
But God is the judge: he putteth down one,
and setteth up another"*
(Psalm 75:6-7 KJV).

You are almost there! Even though this part of the journey is drawing to a close, another exciting part of your journey is just beginning. It is time to talk about your responsibility to others. Now that you are in possession of knowledge that has revolutionized your life, expect God to use you to assist someone else in their pursuit of the Maximized Life.

So you need to know that promotion comes from the Lord and not from man. And one thing is very clear: God wants us to receive every promotion that comes to us. Part of our promotion package is sharing our faith with others: *"Live right, and you will eat from the life-giving tree. And if you act wisely, others will follow"* (Proverbs 11:30 CEV). As a part of your Maximized Life Journey, it is very important that you remember that this journey is not just for you. Everyone who you come in contact with should be affected by your Journey. How this happens is the promotion of a lifestyle and love of Jesus in and around the unsaved, the untaught, the unchurched, and the uncommitted through genuine relationship. Allow the Holy Spirit to coordinate a moment to witness and share the Gospel.

Reaching out to share your faith with others is an established priority of Christianity across denominational lines. So, no matter what your background, sharing your faith is important. Evangelism was modeled by Jesus and is a mandate of Scripture. You serve God through serving others. We must work to overcome the apathy that

Reciprocal Promotion

has infected the Body of Christ, which has made personal evangelism a work for a select chosen few rather than for the masses.

The barriers to this lifestyle must be overcome through intentional and purposeful effort. There are a few mental barriers to this lifestyle, one being the feeble excuse that, since others are not involved in reaching the lost, then it's not important for you to be involved. Imagine if someone had taken that response when you came along. You should act based on convictions, not the persuasion of others.

Another mental barrier is that personal witnessing is clearly seen as an optional, extracurricular activity. In actuality, Christ's last command should be our first concern: *"Go ye therefore, and teach all nations, baptizing them in the name of the Father, and of the Son, and of the Holy Ghost: Teaching them to observe all things whatsoever I have commanded you: and, lo, I am with you always, even unto the end of the world. Amen"* (Matthew 28:19-20 KJV). Here you see that sharing your faith is not optional but an important part of the stewardship of your relationship with Christ.

Most Believers are focused on other things, and sharing their faith is a distraction from their personal agendas. That's why personal evangelism should be a lifestyle. When something is a lifestyle, it comes naturally. In order for something to become a lifestyle, it must be done repetitively. The more you do it, the easier it becomes.

"Jesus replied with a story: 'A Jewish man was traveling on a trip from Jerusalem to Jericho, and he was attacked by bandits. They stripped him of his clothes, beat him up, and left him half dead beside the road. By chance a priest came along. But when he saw the man lying there, he crossed to the other side of the road and passed him by. A

Temple assistant walked over and looked at him lying there, but he also passed by on the other side. Then a despised Samaritan came along, and when he saw the man, he felt compassion for him. Going over to him, the Samaritan soothed his wounds with olive oil and wine and bandaged them. Then he put the man on his own donkey and took him to an inn, where he took care of him. The next day he handed the innkeeper two silver coins, telling him, 'Take care of this man. If his bill runs higher than this, I'll pay you the next time I'm here.' 'Now which of these three would you say was a neighbor to the man who was attacked by bandits?' Jesus asked. The man replied, 'The one who showed him mercy.' Then Jesus said, 'Yes, now go and do the same'" (Luke 10:30-37 NLT). This well-known story of the Good Samaritan sets the example for how you should live your life as a Maximizer. This story shows a Maximizer in action.

Here are a few inspired thoughts from this story that Jesus shared with His disciples. *The insensitivity of others is not an excuse for irresponsibility.* Because others passed by doesn't mean you have to. You are a leader and you only follow those who through faith and patience are inheriting the promises of God. *This man did not allow his schedule to rob him of an opportunity to serve.* Planners, Blackberries, or iPhones instead of obedience to God govern too many people. They even schedule things that should be spontaneous. However, within your scheduling, you should always leave room for interruptions from the Holy Spirit so that you can be used whenever He deems necessary.

In the story, he addressed the man's brokenness without rebuke or ridicule. Many times when people have to address sensitive issues, they are not considerate to the feelings of others. Here the Samaritan gives you an excellent example that you can address the

Reciprocal Promotion

hard cases without making people feel inferior. *He touched him with the hands of compassion and not the hands of duty.* This man did not feel like he was one among many, but the Samaritan made him feel special. He treated him with value by providing quality ministry and medical attention.

He brought him to a safe environment so others could help restore him. The Samaritan did not count his job completed because he passed the wounded man off. He followed through afterwards. You know that it is after the initial acceptance of Christ that people need a solid support system to keep them on track. The Samaritan arranged for future care by making a financial investment in his care. Now this does not mean that you have to give money to everyone; but occasions will rise when you will need to provide more than spiritual care. (But that's okay because you walk in abundance!)

There are several ways to commit your life to this style of living. Be conscious of this responsibility under the Lordship of Christ. Remember not to forget His plan for your life and that your promotion comes through your obedience. You must learn to obey at a not-knowing level. There must be a conviction about your neglect of evangelism. You are led by your convictions; and when you are convicted, you must respond and change. There must be a confession of faith to agree with God to set this course for life. There must be compassion, which is the product of spiritual empowerment for the task. There must be caring; the outpouring of the love that Jesus had for you inspires action. Your caring must be authentic. People recognize insincerity. And they are tired of it. There must be consistency. There must be the persistent commitment to touch others until there are results. Consistency is very important to your entire journey. Without it, you will stop along the way before you reach your destiny. The single characteristic of the successful is consistency. And, finally, there is celebration. In heaven and earth, there is great joy when people are converted.

Your journey is not complete until you lead others to take the same journey that you are on. Therein lies your true prosperity: helping others arrive where you are—or where you are going. The journey is better with others onboard!

Maximized Prayer:

Father, people matter to You and they need to matter to me. I will value people and love them enough to share Your love with them. In Jesus' name, Amen.

Maximizing Moments:

Make a list of people around you who do not know the Lord Jesus.

Begin to confess salvation over their lives and ask God to use you to share with them the Maximized Life Journey.

Maximizing Mantra:

The compassion of Jesus flows from my heart.

NOTES

DAY 52 – PASS IT ON

*"But to all who did accept him and believe in him
he gave the right to become children of God."*
John 1:12 (NCV)

Here you are on the last day! While this is the last reading for the journey, it is really only a launching point for the rest of your life. This book must be a regular part of your library, and you should revisit it at least once a year. You have created a blueprint for your Maximum Life Journey. Now it is time to put it into practice and see new levels of productivity and accomplishment! Your journey, based on purpose, cannot end without you impacting the life of another. You saw yesterday that evangelism must be a lifestyle that you demonstrate daily. Trust God to lead you to people who are ready to respond to His love.

Your Maximized Life Journey is maturing when it cultivates a passion for the lost and hurting. Many people do not actively share their faith because they lack the resolve to practice the simple principles of lifestyle evangelism.

In the ministry of Jesus, people were involved in lifestyle evangelism immediately after being ministered to by Him. Let's look at one such example: *"A crowd soon gathered around Jesus, and they saw the man who had been possessed by the legion of demons. He was sitting there fully clothed and perfectly sane, and they were all afraid. Then those who had seen what happened told the others about the demon-possessed man and the pigs. And the crowd began pleading with Jesus to go away and leave them alone. As Jesus was getting into the boat, the man who had been demon possessed begged to go with him. But Jesus said, 'No, go home to your family, and tell them everything the Lord has done for you and how merciful he has been.' So the man started off to visit the Ten Towns of that region and began to proclaim the great things Jesus had done for him; and everyone was amazed at what he told them"* (Mark 5:15-20 NLT).

This man was able to spread the Gospel to ten (10) cities just from his testimony. This dispels the myth that in order to effectively witness to others you must complete evangelism courses or be formally trained. Your testimony of the goodness of God in your life is sufficient to make an impact on those outside of the faith. A testimony is the simple articulation and affirmation of the grace and goodness of God, which points someone to Jesus.

There is a scriptural pattern for an effective testimony: *"The woman took the hint and left. In her confusion she left her water pot. Back in the village she told the people, 'Come see a man who knew all about the things I did, who knows me inside and out. Do you think this could be the Messiah?' And they went out to see for themselves . . . many of the Samaritans from that village committed themselves to him because of the woman's witness: 'He knew all about the things I did. He knows me inside and out!' They asked him to stay on, so Jesus stayed two days. A lot more people entrusted their lives to him when they heard what he had to say. They said to the woman, 'We're no longer taking this on your say-so. We've heard it for ourselves and know it for sure. He's the Savior of the world!'"* (John 4:28-30, 39-42 MSG). What an amazing testimony! Look at the change that occurred to the entire town from the testimony of this Samaritan woman.

Let's look at the simple profile of an effective testimony. All marketing strategists agree that the best form of advertisement is a word of mouth testimony from a compelling and reliable reference. Your testimony is the claim of divine favor, which both validates the Word of God and acknowledges the faithfulness of God. The formula for personal testimony is in the form of questions. Here are the questions: Where were you when it happened? What was happening? What did God do for you? Who did God use? Where did God lead you? Where are you now? Who do you give the praise to? These are the type of questions that you use to formulate your personal testimony.

Your testimony is yours and no one can tell it like you do. The focus of a personal testimony must be clear. It can't be scrambled and unfocused. It must be clear and consistent. The quickest way to turn people off is when they see inconsistencies in your story. It must be conclusive. Stay away from cliff hangers. By the conclusion of the testimony, people should be given hope. You want to be sure that there is no ambiguity. They should not be wondering what the point of this story is. The testimony should be correct (truthful). It cannot be a sensationalizing of the truth or a complete fabrication. And the final part of the formula for personal testimony is that it must be compelling—just like the Samaritan woman's testimony. After hearing your testimony, people should be able to say, "I heard what you said. How do I experience Him for myself?": *"All Believers, come here and listen, let me tell you what God did for me. I called out to him with my mouth, my tongue shaped the sounds of music. If I had been cozy with evil, the Lord would never have listened. But he most surely did listen, he came on the double when he heard my prayer. Blessed be God: he didn't turn a deaf ear, he stayed with me, loyal in his love"* (Psalm 66:16-20 MSG).

There is a supernatural purpose for an effective testimony. Humans can only communicate the Good News, the Gospel. You were designed to tell of His goodness and His mercy. There are some things that only people can communicate to each other. When there is a need for a contemporary example of ancient truth, your

Reciprocal Promotion

effective testimony has a supernatural purpose. You make what happened in the past relevant to today. The way you communicate makes the story come to life for people who otherwise would have been separated from God. When all of a person's resources are depleted and the person is contemplating giving up, your effective testimony can have a supernatural purpose in the life of that person. You know the power of God and that He is a provider. And perhaps you have experienced His provision in tough times. That testimony will help so many people. When a person is looking for direction, your personal testimony can give them the direction that they so desperately need.

Never despise your testimony, no matter how great or small it may be. You will have many testimonies as you continue on the Maximized Life Journey! Be prepared to share them as milestones to your place of destiny! It's time to pass it on!

Day 52 - Pass It On

Maximized Prayer:

Father, thank You for Your faithfulness in my life. I have many testimonies of Your intervention in my life. My story cannot be told with mentioning You! I commit to be transparent so that others can be blessed by my story. In Jesus' name, Amen.

Maximizing Moments:

Write out the testimony of your life.

Find three (3) significant areas where God has proven Himself for you. Write a short testimony about those times. Then ask God to show you someone with whom to share them.

Maximizing Mantra:

My story will bless the lives of others!

NOTES

Additional Resources

Maximized Life Journey Resources

15 FREEDOM TRUTHS

1. I am a new creation in Christ Jesus predestined for greatness. (2 Corinthians 5:17)
2. I am a child of God fully accepted by the Father. (John 1:12)
3. I am loved by God no matter how I perform. (Romans 5:8)
4. I am forgiven and will not be tormented by my past errors. (1 John 1:9)
5. I am an overcomer and my faith is changing my circumstances. (1 John 5:4)
6. I am a giver and people are looking to bless me and give into my life today. (Luke 6:38; 2 Corinthians 9:5)
7. I have authority over the devil and no demon power can hurt me. (Luke 10:17)
8. Abundance is God's will for me and I will not settle for less. (John 10:10)
9. I am healed and sickness will not Lord it over my body. (1 Peter 2:24)
10. God is on my side and I will not fear. (Psalm 118:6)
11. The Holy Spirit is my helper; I am never alone and I have the peace of God. (Philippians 4:7)
12. I am blessed and it's a matter of time before things change. What I see is temporary. (Ephesians 1:3; 2 Corinthians 4:18)
13. I have the wisdom of God; I hear the Father's voice; my steps are ordered by God and the voice of a stranger I will not follow. (1 Corinthians 1:30)
14. I am set in the body of Christ and I know that I am valuable and important to the work of God. (1 Corinthians 12:20-25)
15. I choose not to be offended and I am being delivered out of all afflictions and persecutions. (Matthew 5:1-12)

CONFESSION FOR OVERCOMING WORRY, STRESS AND SLEEPLESSNESS

Father, I commit every anxiety, every worry and every care to You, and I receive your peace that rules my heart and my mind. My heart and mind are fixed on You, therefore, I have perfect peace.

When I lie down my sleep is sweet and I have peace and safety. I am Your beloved and You promised Your beloved sweet rest. Thank you!

Father, in the name of Jesus, I thank you that I have great peace and because I love the Word nothing shall offend me. Thank You Lord, when I lie down I receive blessings from You. I choose to cast every anxious thought on You because I know you care for me.

CONFESSION FOR HUSBANDS

Father, in the name of Jesus, I embrace the truth of Your Word and commit it to my life. I commit to change whatever needs to be changed in my life in order to bring every thought into captivity to Your Word and will for my life.

I am a mighty man of valor and I see my wife as a virtuous woman. I love my wife as Your Son loved the church. The light of Your Word shines on my path. My heart safely trusts in my wife. She is good to me and she is good for me. I place high value on her. She is precious to me. My wife is spiritually focused, emotionally strong, and she has unquestionable character.

Father, in Jesus' name, if I have damaged my wife through selfishness, deep-rooted or misguided expectations, or my carelessness, I commit to make restitution. I will help her develop as a person and I will let her help me. I will shine on her as the sun shines on the earth. I bring her warmth, nurture, protection and security.

I gladly drink of the cup that was prepared before we married because it brings us joy. I will gladly bear the cross of our relationship and allow my wife to be herself. Today, I die to the things that are destroying our relationship. Everyday we experience a new creation marriage where old things are passed away and all things are become new.

Maximized Life Journey Resources

CONFESSION FOR WIVES

Father, I thank you that I am a capable, intelligent, virtuous woman and the heart of my husband does safely trust in me so that he has no need of spoil. I do my husband good all the days of his life. I respect my husband as a man of God and I always speak good things about him to others. When I embarrass and speak negatively about my husband it is rottenness in his bones. So, I choose to speak only good things about him and our relationship.

I am a good thing that my husband has found and because of me he has obtained favor of the Lord. My husband dwells with me according to knowledge and he gives honor to me as unto the weaker vessel. My husband loves me as Christ loves the church.

My husband and I have wonderful, intimate times together because my breasts satisfy him at all times and he is ravished with my love. We render to one another due benevolence.

My children and my husband rise and call me blessed. I live the overcoming life. I live in daily expectation of abundance in my life. I have a sound mind and I live a life of purpose and fulfillment. I am a blessing to my household and to the kingdom of God.

I love my husband and do him good all the days of our lives. God satisfies us with long life and peace. My husband is known in the gates (city, state, nation and abroad) and when he sits with kings, rulers and high officials, he gives wise counsel. His gift makes room for him and brings him before great men.

Lord, you promised to perfect all that concerns me and I am thankful.

Maximized Life Journey Resources

CONFESSION FOR SINGLES

Jesus Christ is Lord over my spirit, soul and my body. I am a child of God, loved by my Father. I live the victorious and overcoming life. And, every need in my life is met.

I choose to walk in the Spirit therefore I have life and peace. The lust of my flesh has no power over me because the Holy Spirit leads and guides me into all truth. My steps are ordered by God.

God is preparing the perfect mate for me and when the Spirit of God causes our paths to cross, I have favor in his/her eyes. I choose to keep myself holy until marriage.

I walk in divine health. Sickness and disease have no place in my body because I'm covered by the blood of Jesus. I only think those things that are true, honest, pure and of good report. I am committed to seeking God, consistently and regularly, because He is a rewarder of the diligent.

I spend quality time helping others in the kingdom of God and I am involved in my local church because this is the blessed state. In Jesus' name, I walk by faith and not by sight.

Maximized Life Journey Resources

PROSPERITY CONFESSION OF THE GIVER

Father, in the name of Jesus, I confess Your Word over my finances this day. I have given the tithes of my increase and I now receive the window of heaven blessing on my life. Thank You Father. I have the mind of Christ and am obedient to You because I trust You. My mind is alert, and I hear Your voice. The voice of the stranger I will not follow. Thank You, I receive now doors of opportunity opening for me, and my family.

Father, I have given to the poor; therefore, I will never lack. I always have all sufficiency in all things as You are raising up others to use their power, ability and influence to help me. I expect Your Spirit to speak daily to men and women concerning giving to me. In the name of Jesus, those whom the Spirit of God designates are now free to obey and give to me good measure, pressed down, shaken together and running over.

In Jesus' name, I believe every need is met with heaven's best. I have given for the support of the man and woman of God who teach me the Word. They have sown into my life that which is spiritual; according to Your Word, and I have sown into their lives that which is natural. You promised that you would supply all my needs according to Your riches in glory by Christ Jesus. Thank you Father, I live in the best, I wear the best, I drive the best, I eat the best, and I go first class in life.

Father, your Word also says I can decree a thing because of my covenant vow with You for the kingdom of God in the earth. This is my decree and I thank You for wisdom and insight to bring it to pass. You give me, and my family richly all things to enjoy. satan, I bind your activity in my life and I loose the angels, the ministering spirits, to minister for me and bring the necessary finances so that I may continue to finance the kingdom of God.

Father, Your Word declares that my giving increases the fruit of my righteousness. I thank you Father that I have an abundance of peace, joy, patience, temperance and goodness. The optimum return on my giving is mine because I have given to promote the name of Jesus and the Gospel.